WITHDRA

D0853727

An
Uncommon
Sailor

An Uncommon Sailor

A PORTRAIT OF ADMIRAL SIR WILLIAM PENN
English Naval Supremacy

Lucie Street

St. Martin's Press
New York

AN UNCOMMON SAILOR. Copyright © 1988 by Lucie Street. All rights reserved. Printed in the United States of America. No part of this book may be used or reproduced in any manner whatsoever without written permission except in the case of brief quotations embodied in critical articles or reviews. For information, address St. Martin's Press, 175 Fifth Avenue, New York, N.Y. 10010.

Library of Congress Cataloging-in-Publication Data

Street, Lucie.
    An uncommon sailor : a portrait of Sir William Penn / by Lucie
Street.
        p.   cm.
    ISBN 0-312-01526-7 : $12.95 (est.)
    1. Penn, William, Sir, 1621–1670.   2. Admirals—Great Britain-
-Biography.   3. Great Britain. Royal Navy—Biography.   4. Great
Britain—History, Naval—Stuarts, 1603–1714.   I. Title.
DA86.1.P4S77 1988
941.06′092′4—dc19
    [B]   87-27109
                                                                          CIP

First published in Great Britain by The Kensal Press

First U.S. Edition

10   9   8   7   6   5   4   3   2   1

Contents

Frontis. Admiral Sir William Penn. *National Maritime Museum.*

Preface and Acknowledgements

I am deeply indebted to Lord Maybray-King, the former Speaker, who introduced me to Mr John Palmer, Chief Librarian of the Home and Parliamentary Affairs Section Research Division and asked him to send me details about Penn's service as M.P. for Weymouth and Melcombe Regis. Mr Palmer did a great deal more than this, including facts concerning the admiral's greatest friend, Admiral Sir William Batten, and others, as well as introducing me to helpful sources in the Caribbean, and often answering difficult queries concerning the period of my study. Mr Maurice Bond, E.B.E., Clerk to the House of Lords Record Office, and Mr. H. S. Cobb, Deputy Clerk of the Records, greatly helped me in my searches in the *Journals of the House of Commons* and the *Journals of the House of Lords* and explained what otherwise I would have missed. Dame Veronica Wedgwood, O.M., has throughout been kindness itself both in conversations and in letters.

Sir Eric Penn, O.B.E., Controller of the Lord Chamberlain's Office at St James' Palace, provided an introduction to the Resident Governor and Keeper of the Jewel House, Queen's House, H.M. Tower of London, Major General W. D. M. Raebury, C.B., who invited me to the Tower and spent most of one morning giving me the history of the buildings as they were in the time of Admiral Penn, with the plans and many engravings. What he told me proved part of my thesis beyond any doubt whatsoever.

Then followed help from A. V. B. Norman, Master Armourer, Tower of London. As to the navy itself, I must first thank Admiral David Kirke for an introduction to the First Sea Lord, after which Rear-Admiral Buckley, C.B., of the Ministry of Defence Library, allowed me to study in the precincts. The Second Sea Lord, Vice-Admiral Empson, Chief of Naval Personnel, spoke of the British Maritime Museum at Greenwich with its famous library of naval records, books and papers, including, as I knew, those private naval papers of Admiral Penn donated a century ago by the Penn family. The Librarian, Dr M. W. B. Sanderson, produced other original documents concerning Admiral Penn, engraved on sheepskin. My thanks are also due to the Deputy Keeper of MSS, Dr Roger Knight. The Head of Department of Ships, Mr A. P. McGowan, brought the past to life by showing the original models of ships from which the navy in Admiral Penn's time was built, before drawings were used. I am indebted to the Flag-Admiral of the Medway who suggested a visit to Chatham Dockyard where Lieutenant-Commander E. Crittenden of H.M. Naval Base, Chatham, took me round the historic parts of the dockyard and explained it in much detail, even down to the 'Ropery' as it is used today unchanged. I must thank Mrs Goldsworthy, Deputy Civil Secretary, Port Admiral's Office, Chatham, for her arrangements for me. There is also the Warden of Upnor Castle to thank, Mr John Windle, who knew the history of every stone and every gun including those now missing which faced across to the Medway; also the carpenter there, Mr Daunt. At Gillingham Public Library, the Librarian, Mr Tomlinson, was steeped in local history. The disgrace of the Medway disaster is felt to this day by all these gentlemen.

Lord Hacking of Hemel Hempstead must be thanked for introducing me to Mr R. C. Latham, Fellow and Pepys Librarian of Magdalene College, Cambridge, who placed his knowledge and books at my disposal, as well as showing the one great Penn treasure the Pepys Library possesses: the bound copy of Admiral Penn's letters owned by Charles II. All this made for unforgettable days. I am also indebted to Mr Bernard Braithwaite of Cambridge, Adviser to the World Bank in Education, who did much to make my stay useful in general studies.

The Society of Merchant Venturers, Merchants' Hall, Bristol, allowed me into their building filled with treasures, after the City Archivist, Miss Williams, had vouched for me. My gratitude to the members of the staff whom I met is beyond expression. Miss Morris and Mrs Patience Brewer themselves looked through their seventeenth-century records on my behalf and Mrs Brewer continued to post me further extracts from the Society of Merchant Venturers' Book of Trade (1598–1693) as and when she found them. I was allowed to study the Deposition Books of Bristol 1643–1647 – together with 'Merchants and Merchandise in Seventeenth Century Bristol' as well as John Latimer's 'Calendar of Records' and countless other documents not available elsewhere, but all of which reflected matters affecting the trade of Captain Giles Penn, Admiral Penn's father, as well as his brother and uncle. I am also much indebted to Miss Judith Smith, Church Archivist of St Thomas the Martyr and of St Mary Redcliffe and the Chief Verger who had to be present when the safes were unlocked to examine the deeds of marriages and burials, and ancient churchwarden's accounts.

Sir Lawrence Lindo, the then High Commissioner for Jamaica in London, greatly helped by his introduction to the Governor General, Sir Florizel Glasspole, who himself furthered my requests for historical help. Sir Lawrence Lindo had already written to Mr Bernard Lewis, Director of the Institute of Jamaica; to Clinton Black, the Archivist for Jamaica, and to Shirley Mayner Burke of the Institute of Jamaica and West India Library. The file may not have been large, but it yielded riches which greatly rewarded the flight across the Atlantic. To these names must be added that of Dr Elsa Waters, formerly at the University of Jamaica.

To the historian, J. R. Powell, specialist on Blake and the civil war and the navy, I am also indebted for original material as well as for his introduction to the Librarian of the University of Kent at Canterbury, Mr C. S. Darlow, who produced a book of which I was in desperate need. I must also record thanks to Miss Sonia Anderson, English National Register of Archivists and a Member of the Historical Commission; also to Miss B. L. Bell, the County Archivist at Bedford, who produced the private deeds of landed property of the Penn family.

The Religious Society of Friends have a library in the Euston Road, London, and the Chief Librarian, Edward H. Milligan, found valuable notes not elsewhere obtainable. In Ireland the Society of Friends, in the persons of Ivan and Myrtle Allen, gave unpublished records of activities concerning the Penn family as well as the Friends' publication *Memorial to William Penn in Ireland*.

In the public library at Limerick, the Librarian speeded photostats to save me several journeys and at Bunratty Castle everyone was anxious to help. In particular Mr Christopher Lynch, Manager of Bunratty Castle, Mr Tom Sheeds, Assistant Manager, and Mr Philip Quigley, Assistant Keeper of the Cast.

At Weymouth, I was particularly fortunate to find Lieutenant-Commander Ian Hewitt, R.N., who was stationed there at the time and explained a great deal about the sailing difficulties around Portland

Bill due to cross currents, strong tides, and Chesil Beach, all hazards in the time of Admiral Penn and not to be despised today. To him and Mrs Hewitt I owe much hospitality as well as visits to the naval mess, with the sea roaring below. The Librarian of Weymouth Public Library, Mr J. A. C. West, was proud to show an original letter from Jamaica in Admiral Penn's own handwriting and also many illustrations of naval dress at that time.

Admiral Penn's son, William, spent ten years at Chigwell Grammar School. This country village was small but its Grammar School was already famous and today its old buildings remain unchanged, so that I am deeply indebted to the Headmaster, Mr B. J. Wilson, and Mr Salmon, the School Librarian, for the time spent showing the actual classrooms where William Penn learned to read before going up into the 'Latin School'. Also to Mr Eric Crabbe for his introduction to these gentlemen.

No list of authors' thank-yous can ever be complete without mention made of the Chief Librarian of the London Library, Mr Stanley Gillam, and his learned and helpful staff who are never at a loss when difficult points arise. To them, my thanks are heartfelt indeed.

Then there is the Society of Authors and their qualified staff who are always at hand to members when advice and help is needed, and I am especially grateful to Mr George Astley and Miss Philippa MacLeish.

Last, but not least, is my daughter-in-law, the Australian composer, who composes under her maiden name of Jenifer Fowler. Her patience in reading and annotating every reference to the name of Penn in all eleven volumes of *The Diary of Samuel Pepys,* edited by R. C. Latham and W. Matthews, saved me many hours. The problem was that I had worked on Wheatley's standard edition of 1893, which I found in the Naval Ministry of Defence Library at Fulham, and built up my thesis on Samuel Pepys' relations with the Admiral and their effort on his life from the edition. I hoped nothing of importance had been missed in my work as these splendid new volumes appeared. Fortunately no changes or additions had to be made.

Whatever is of value in this book is entirely due to the ungrudging help of the above experts in so many fields of knowledge and it would be wrong to pretend otherwise.

Lucie Street
Warminghurst 1986

Introduction

Today, Admiral Sir William Penn is most often remembered as the father of the founder of Pennsylvania. Yet the establishment of that colony owed as much to the achievement of the father as to the visionary perseverance of the son. Indeed, the territory was granted by the crown chiefly as a thank-offering for the admiral's naval services. 'Whereas his Majesty,' said the letters patent conferring the grant,

> in consideration of the merit and faithful services of Sir William Penn, deceased, and for divers other good causes him thereto moving, hath been graciously pleased . . . to give and grant unto William Penn, all that tract or land in America, called by the name of Pennsylvania, . . . his Majesty does therefore hereby publish and declare his royal will and pleasure, that all persons settled or inhabiting within the limits of the said province, do yield all due obedience to the said William Penn.

Charles II enclosed his grant in a letter to the admiral's son, which explained that the gesture of royal munificence was made 'for the merit and Memory of Sir W. Penn and particularly his conduct, discretion and courage under our dearest brother the Duke of York', in the Second Dutch War.

Nor was Pennsylvania the only late fruit of Admiral Penn's career. The purpose of this brief memoir is to show that Penn should be ranked with Drake and Nelson as one of the great makers of the English naval tradition, outstanding in his care of ships and men, brilliantly innovative in tactics and strategy. Victories and long-term accretions of English naval strength in his day, often attributed to Blake or even to Monck or the Duke of York, should in justice be ascribed to Penn. Above all, the wresting of naval supremacy from the Dutch was, I hope to suggest, Penn's work, rather than that of any other individual. The consequence of that adjustment in the naval balance of power was enshrined in the Treaty of Breda of 1661: the Atlantic seaboard of North

America – notwithstanding Dutch gains elsewhere – became wholly and inviolably English. In the land which was to perpetuate Penn's name, English traditions were sewn, never to be uprooted. More generally, all the common experiences and common culture on which England's friendship with America is founded, stem from the Treaty of Breda. In the forging of England's maritime greatness, in the transmission of the English heritage overseas, Admiral Sir William Penn occupies a cardinal place in history. It is time for that place to be celebrated and, we may hope, widely acknowledged.

Why has Penn's role been so long belittled or overlooked? Part of the answer lies in the very modesty with which he avoided public praise and effaced his own achievement in despatches. Yet the emulous Restoration court was no place to be modest in, without sacrifice of fame. For Penn was a victim of terrible political jealousies. In the last years of his life, as we shall see, Monck and Prince Rupert manoeuvred him out of command, and Clarendon succeeded almost in expunging him from the historical record. Penn attracted all this illustrious odium for the most innocent of reasons. His unexcelled naval experience made him, as Pepys remarked, 'fitter for command than anybody else'; his effective position at the head of the Restoration navy gave him the companionship and confidence – and therefore the coveted patronage – of the heir to the throne. He seemed poised to occupy the position of *eminence grise* which his rivals felt was theirs: Monck, as the self-appointed kingmaker of the Restoration; Rupert, as the king's cousin and the royal family's longest-serving defender; Clarendon as the royal 'uncle', father-in-law to the heir. Clarendon's own history of his times, more than any other, has influenced – indeed, has formed – the subsequent historiographical tradition. Thus, suppressed in Clarendon's account, Penn's part was omitted from the books derived from it. Only assiduous research in archival material, or in contemporary pamphlets long buried in libraries, would have dispelled the darkness to which Penn's reputation was consigned. In some degree, as we shall see, Penn was also undone by his own disinterested patriotism. Never a republican at heart, he leapt to England's defence against external enemies, whatever the régime. As a result, despite strong evidence of his loyalty, the cavaliers never fully trusted him. Modesty and patriotism: never, perhaps, was man so much the victim of his virtues.

Penn was re-discovered in the nineteenth century following the emergence from obscurity of Pepys's *Diary*. Yet, even in this, the admiral was unlucky. Pepys shared his own patrons' jealousy of Penn, who so greatly outshone his own 'protector' – his uncle, and Penn's close comrade in arms and in parliament, the Earl of Sandwich. Pepys and Penn were colleagues on the Navy Board, neighbours in Navy Gardens, daily playgoers, diners and carousers together, companions in many sallies against hostile parliamentary committees or against what would now be called 'defence cuts'. Still, those bonds of friendship did not deter Pepys from traducing Penn in the *Diary* and accussing him repeatedly of vulgarity, ignorance and dishonesty. These charges, though untrue, have stuck in many historians' perceptions of Penn. Yet contemplation of the admiral's papers shows a man of considerable intellect and broad culture. Consideration of his career suggests standards of uncompromising probity in a corrupt age. Indeed, it is hard to resist the impression that it was Penn's avowed role as a watchdog over peculation and graft of the Navy Board which most annoyed Pepys. And even Pepys, be it noted, acknowledged the admiral's professional gifts and superior qualifications for command. Eight years after the *Diary* appeared, Penn's great-grandson Granville, tried to set the record straight by publishing the ships' logs and the official reports of battles. But this book was technical, prolix, uninvitingly corpulent and vulnerable to charges of special pleading. It was soon forgotten, while Pepys's brilliant, excoriating, scabrous prose was read with delight by every generation.

Save for inaccessible contemporary pamphlets, and indigestible family piety, the only work in print which did justice to Penn's achievement was a French naval training textbook. Paul Hoste, Professor of Mathematics in the Royal Seminary of Toulon, illustrated his 'System of Sea-Discipline' with examples from 'the most remarkable sea-engagements between England and Holland'. He was an enemy subject; so his impartiality is assured. From his pages, Penn's contribution to the establishment of English naval supremacy can be inferred. Hoste argued that Penn had created a revolutionary tactical system and applied it in his two great victories off the Texel. Previously, opposing naval forces had sailed abreast, their keels parallel, engaged in individual combat. Penn ordered his ships to sail in line through the enemy's centre, doubling their broadsides and rounding on the foe from behind. The book's status as a training manual ensured the transmission of Penn's tactics; among Hoste's readers was Nelson; among the battles fought in the same tradition was Trafalgar. The English naval tradition remains strong today, strong in some of the qualities Penn helped to give it. English naval supremacy, which Penn helped to found, may be a thing of the past, but it has been one of the most significant and long-enduring features of modern history. It is a proper matter of regret that Penn's own fame has not survived, in its due place, alongside.

CHAPTER ONE

The Young Captain

The exact date of William Penn's birth is unknown, but his baptism occurred at a time of favourable auspices on 23rd April, 1621. The choice of St George's Day was peculiarly fitting for an infant who would grow into a redoubtable defender of England's shores and who would, in manhood, make a fundamental, albeit generally unacknowledged, contribution to the foundations of England's national greatness. 1621 was not exactly an *annus mirabilis:* perhaps the most distinguished of Penn's contemporaries were Andrew Marvell and one of Cromwell's sons. But it was the year of the establishment of the precarious colony founded in America by the fathers of the *Mayflower,* of the resumption of religious strife in the Netherlands, and of the irreversible exacerbation of the Thirty Years War. These facts between them convey a flavour of the time: of civil discord and religious dissent, of danger and creativity and adventure.

William Penn was born into a seafaring family, in a great port with a distinguished maritime tradition. Bristol merchants had been active in the Levant and all over the north Atlantic since the late fifteenth century. The Mediterranean, full of hostile vested interests, was at first reluctant to admit interlopers from the north, but in the late sixteenth century shortages of shipping and dearth of grain induced a new mood of guarded hospitality, which the more far-sighted and enterprising of the Bristol men were able to exploit. Specialisation in the Mediterranean trade became a common livelihood in Bristol. The Penn family were latecomers to this world. If a tradition established by the son of Pennsylvanias's founder may be trusted, they can be traced with some confidence to David Penn, lord of the manor of Penn in the county of Buckinghamshire, who, in the reign of Henry VIII married Sybil, daughter of William Hampden of Kimble. This union, of two families whose names would become famous as symbols of the defence and spread of English traditions of liberty, prospered and bore fruit. Sybil was chosen to take care of the king's motherless heir after the death of Jane Seymour and the favour she thus incurred proved the making of her younger son, William. Allegedly a monk of Glastonbury at the time of the dissolution of the monasteries, he was plucked from the debacle by the grace of a grateful king and installed in an estate, carved from the holdings of his erstwhile abbey, at Minety in the Forest of Bradon, Wiltshire. Small local offices of profit under the crown enhanced the status and income of his descendants, but younger sons had to look elsewhere for a role. Thus the two cadets of the fourth generation of the Penns of Minety removed to Bristol and beyond, in the trade of merchant venturers.

Of the junior partner in this fraternal enterprise little more is known, save his name: he was another William. But the senior, Giles, rapidly established himself as a merchant of substance and a man of consequence. His business at Leghorn, Cadiz, Sanqúcar de Barrameda and Seville was extensive. It extended into the Marinid sultanate, and it brought Giles to a thorough mastery of seamanship. He was no shore-bound capitalist, but an active trader and ship's master, who trained his sons in the same arts. The elder son, George, was already grown to manhood when the younger, William, was born; the future admiral thus spent his early years chiefly in his mother's company, during the men's long absences at sea: the experience left him with – perhaps gave him – a love of his kin and of closely united family life which he was to show in all his future conduct. But it seems that he lost no time in following his father and brother to sea: it was probably William's early start in sea-faring, at the age of twelve, that provided the foundation of the myth that he was an 'ignorant tarpaulin', raised from a cabin boy. His father may well have set him to learn the ways of a ship from the bottom up: cleaning the galley, climbing the masts, later graduating to a post behind the helmsman on the next-to-top deck, looking up through the square hole cut in the ceiling to watch the sails belly out in the wind, and pulling at the whipstaff: there was no wheel to steer by on seventeenth-century ships.

The fiercest blight on Giles Penn's trade was the hostility of the Barbary corsairs. Every Maghribi port was a lair of pirates and slavers who lived by raiding the southern shores of Christendom and preying on peaceful commerce. They throve on plunder and ransom. As his father's agent in Seville and Cadiz, for instance, George Penn must soon have become thoroughly acquainted with their depredations. In 1609, fourteen-year-old Diego Rodríguez was captured in Mijas, several miles inland from Marbella. In 1610, Juan Rodríguez of Granada was captured while travelling by land from Almeria to Cartagena. In 1613, the herdsman Juan González was seized at Casabermeja, about thirty kilometres inland from Málaga. In 1637, Calpe in Valencia was razed to the ground by the corsairs. These incidents were thoroughly typical. The Moors helped themselves to ships at sea, in the Mediterranean and Atlantic alike; they raided the coasts, struck inland and surprised their victims literally in sleep or at mass.

While England was not directly exposed to the *razzie* of the corsairs, England's ships were vulnerable whenever they strayed into the sort of latitudes frequented by the house of Penn. By 1636, a thousand Englishmen were thought to be rotting in dungeons or chained to oars in Salah alone. Though ransom remained the established means of procuring the liberty of such captives, the scale of the problem seemed to call for extraordinary action. When a punitive expedition was mooted, the man commissioned to lead it had to be chosen for his knowledge of the hostile waters. Few captains in the regular naval service can have known much about Morocco; but Giles Penn, from long acquaintance, had invaluable expertise. With a commission from the king, Captain Penn was appointed to command His Majesty's squadron against the 'heathen Moors of Sallee'. The expedition was a triumph: Salah was blockaded and 339 English captives disgorged under Captain Penn's guns. It is likely that young William was not allowed to take part in such a dangerous adventure, but he reaped a share of its glory. For the following year, 1637, when his father was rewarded with the king's warrant to be consul at Salah, William shipped on board as second-in-command. On arrival in Salah, when his father disembarked to take up the consulship, William inherited the vacant bridge: in February, 1638, at only seventeen years, he was master of his own ship.

No log survives from this first command. But from the time of year, the circumstances of the voyage and the known facts of William's early training and later record, a few inferences can be safely drawn. Though young, Penn was no ingénue. Mutual trust with his crew was already founded on a long record of common endeavour. He had grown up with his men. They had taught him. He had fed with them, raced them up the rigging, stood with them at the guns and seen their comrades die at his side. In an age when, at least in English practice, it was common for landlubbers to exercise naval commands, Penn was distinguished not only by his long apprenticeship in his craft but also by his compassionate understanding of the service. It is tempting to try to reconstruct imaginatively his feelings on his first independent command. He must have walked along the 'Admiral's promenade', the private gangway running round the stern, high above the water. The view was commanding. The bow of the ship was low and sharp-pointed to cut clean through the waves, but the stern was built high, deck above deck, for the captain's office, his cabin and the officers' dining room. While the men lived below in near darkness, direction came from the loftiest part of the stern, where the captain could observe the performance of the sails, the deployment of the men and the imminence of danger. Did the young William find that solitary eminence awesome or comforting, exhilarating or intimidating? The balance of probabilities is that, as he was very much in his element and well prepared for responsibility, he was planning – and perhaps practising – the characteristic methods of his early years of command. We can picture him glancing up the rigging and resolving to spend more time on sail drill than his father, cutting the time taken by a full two minutes and increasing the safety along with the speed. More men were lost at sea by injuries during sail-changing than from hostile action, disease or any other cause. No power on earth could prevent such accidents but practice might diminish them. Penn's concern was inspired by fellow-feeling with his crew, no doubt, but he had a merchant's awareness of the need for a full, healthy and well disposed complement of men. His hatred of suffering and his anxiety for efficiency were compatible – indeed, complementary – feelings.

Scanning the ship, scrutinising the men, his eyes would also linger on the horizon. The greatest danger would come when they were level with the Straits of Gibraltar, for it was almost spring: the voyage home began in February, and the time was at hand for the Barbary pirates to leave their winter quarters and attack; later, Penn became a remarkable tactical innovator: it is reasonable to suppose that from early in his career he relished combat and pondered its possibilities. He already knew, at all costs, to keep his ship to windward when his guns fired on the foe; but there were two outstanding problems which no known technique satisfactorily solved. The guns' limited range and the difficulty of getting them to bear on the enemy hampered a ship's effectiveness in action. The maximum angle any ship could get from its rudder, when manoeuvring for a broadside, was twenty degrees, and even this was available only to large vessels. One day, Penn would have larger ships to command, and would be in a position to order cannon of superior range: that much he must have been able to foresee even on his first command. Whether he yet had any inkling of how the problems could be solved by tactical initiative is an intriguing but unanswerable question.

One principle of his nautical life which was already to fore of Penn's mind was expressed in his oft-recalled family motto: *Dum Clavum Teneam.* Translated into nautical terms, 'While I hold the key' might be rendered 'While I am in command, I steer a firm course.' On his first command, with a good south-west trade wind blowing west of Ushant, his best course might have borne him back to England in one month.

* * *

For a while after his father entered royal service, young Penn plied the family trade, frequenting Rotterdam and making at least one extensive voyage through the Mediterranean. He took out cargoes of iron and tin, red Bristol cloth, Yorkshire textiles and whites, and brought back spices, currants, raisins, Malaga wine, tapestries, silks, velvets, daggers and knives. The motives and circumstances of his leaving commerce for the Royal Navy are obscure, but the decision can be understood, and even tentatively dated if it is set in the context of the history of the navy and of the development of Penn's own trajectory of life. The former is a story of decadence, which demanded men of Penn's calibre and commitment to right it; the latter of conquest by two forces – both spiritual or sentimental, the one sobering, the other intoxicating – which Penn found irresistible and which determined the course of the rest of his life: moral high-seriousness and love.

The navy had come to a sorry pass. The defeat of the Armada, the triumphs of Drake, Frobisher, Hawkins, Howard and Grenville were easy to recall but impossible to emulate. James 1, short of money and committed to the pursuit of peace, had allowed the ships to dwindle and deteriorate. In 1619 the Venetian ambassador told the Signoria of Venice, with typically merciless candour, 'For the sixteen years that he has been king of England, they have never knocked a nail into any of the royal ships.' The service was correspondingly undervalued under the Stuart regime. Whereas Elizabeth had been proud of her famous seamen and encouraged the affrays which so enriched her coffers, James restrained their zeal. Dampened ardour meant diminished morale. And while the Elizabethan navy was largely staffed and to a great degree led by professional or practical sailors, James – inaugurating a trend that was to prevail for much of the seventeenth century – reserved high naval office and rank for political favourites and court sinecurists. The consequence was neglect, not only of the ships but also of the seamen. In December, 1625, after the English debacle at Cadiz, the *Swiftsure* was used as a hospital ship to bring men home. St Leger wrote to Conway, 'Their state is most miserable . . . the soldiers are sick and naked.' Three years later, when Penn was seven years old, Sir Henry Morton reported to the Lord High Admiral, 'For want of clothes men are so exposed to the weather that their toes and feet rot and fall away piecemeal.'

By the death of James I, the navy had attained the nadir. The new king, Charles I, was more interested and better disposed: indeed, by comparison, his reign would become an age of opportunity for seamen. The high priority accorded to the navy and the high status assigned to men connected with the service are exemplified by the case of Phineas Pett, the naval architect who was to rebuilt English naval power. His portrait hangs in the Maritime Museum Greenwich, in the same room as that of Charles I, while Penn and the other admirals dance attendance in the adjoining gallery: this arrangement evokes the lifetime relationship of the shipbuilder and his patron. In the close, friendly and relatively informal court of Charles I, men who could contribute to England's re-armament, in whatever capacity, could enjoy access to the king. But at first, lack of funds impeded naval reconstruction: the Dutch had laughed openly at their massacre of the English at Amboina in 1623, confident of England's impotence to respond. New investment in shipbulding was, indeed, the only available response, and Charles resolved to make an effort on an unprecedented scale. The *Sovereign of the Seas* was built to be the cynosure of its age; it was to serve as a model for all first-rate ships until the time of the ironclads. Ships in those days were built not from drawings but from models and the four foot-long version of *Sovereign of the Seas* now treasured in the Maritime Museum is the very model which Pett carried upstream to Hampton Court for the king's approval in 1634. The hull is made of fine wooden slats through which the whole of the interior is clearly visible. When the model was being transposed, at Woolwich, onto the scale of the greatest warship of the day, the king took his judges to see the work in progress. The sight helped to convince them in favour of authorising the collection of Ship Money.

Ship Money really was used for ship building. The king's willingness to risk his throne by reviving this hated prerogative tax shows the degree of his commitment to re-armament. Yet re-armament alone does not create the most favourable conditions for naval service: in the seventeenth century, nothing aroused naval prospects like a war or the rumour of war. Advancement and enrichment depended alike on victories and prize-taking. While England was at peace, there was little incentive for a man like William Penn to abandon commerce in favour of the navy. Towards the end of the 1630s, however, and early in the 1640s it seemed increasingly likely that war on one front or another was becoming unavoidable. On the one hand, there was a risk of involvement in the continuing Thirty Years' War, in which it seemed at different times that England might become imbroiled on either side. On the other hand, domestic conflict also threatened. No one foresaw a civil war between king and parliament, but Scotland erupted into revolt in 1638 as a result of the king's insistence on reducing the Kirk to Laudian anglicanism. Then, in 1641, the navy was suddenly projected into new importance by the outbreak of religious war in Ireland. On the night of 23rd October the Irish catholic confederates massacred two thousand protestant settlers without warning. Hundreds escaped the 'plantations' – Penn's future wife among them – and fled to England. Horror at the news of rebellion and massacre swept court and country. The Irish – wrote the king to the Commons – 'must be put down with a sharp war, the conducting and prosecution of which be wholly committed to their care and wisdom for carrying it out'. A small Irish squadron was put to sea to prevent foreign help from reaching the rebels.

The formation of the squadron may have been the occasion of William Penn's recruitment to the navy. Though detailed records were not kept before 1660, Penn's service is documented from 1642, when he was made a captain: this implies that he had already served as a lieutenant, as, indeed, his commemorative monument in the Church of St Mary Redcliffe, Bristol, confirms. The Irish squadron, like all forces levied to meet sudden emergencies, included armed merchant ships of twenty-eight to forty guns, taken onto the king's service for the duration of the campaign. In similar circumstances, Penn's father had been drafted for naval duty at the capture of Salah. With a brother at hand to carry on the family business, young William was free to take a similar opportunity if he wished.

At about this time, he was acquiring a more personal interest in the affairs of Ireland. The date of the beginning of his courtship is not known, and he may have espoused the cause of the Irish protestants before espousing one of their daughters. In any event, not more than a few months can have separated the two commitments. Margaret van den Schuren was a gay widow who had lived on her estates near Bunratty until expelled by the Irish Catholic terror. Her father, John Baptist Jasper, merchant of the Strand, who was later to figure as a prolific purchaser of sequestrated royal goods, was evidently a man of means and may have been among the leading London merchants who, we are told, recommended Giles Penn for the consulship of Salah. The families of Penn and Jasper were mutually acquainted, in all probability, for much of Margaret's young widowhood. The evidence of her Irish posessions is unequivocal, because, ten years after the marriage, Penn petitioned for the restitution of his wife's estates in County Clare, Rineanna and Jasper's Bridge, which she had lost on her flight to England during 'the late horrid rebellion'. It was, perhaps, Margaret's return to London that gave romance a chance to blossom. In 1642, Penn was on leave in the capital and it was natural for Jasper to invite the young captain to his house. The couple were drawn to each other by common traits, later depicted with savage brilliancy by Pepys. The foundation of their common feeling, to judge from the notorious *Diary,* was a ribald sense of humour. Penny's jokes included drinking the susceptible into a stupour, singing bawdy songs and supping at midnight off bread-and-butter on the roof. His wife's pranks included flinging Pepys upon a bed at a party and heaping female guests upon him. Until the disappointments of later life turned them into a sorry couple, Pepys found Penn 'a very merry fellow' with a well matched wife.

They were married in the church at St Martin-within-Ludgate, London. The entry reads: '1643. June 6th. Williame Penne and Margaret van der Schuren, by Dr Dyke, Lecturer. . . witness Mr Roch, churchwarden then.' There is a second certificate of marriage, which may have been needed for Penn's claim for the return of his wife's estates in Ireland, because the given date is confirmed by the register still in existence in the Guildhall, in the City of London, where it is written in a bold hand under the year 1643: 'June 6. William Penne and Margaret van der Schuren by Mr Dyke, Lecturer.' Miraculously, that register escaped both the Fire of London in 1666 and the blitz, when the Guildhall was destroyed by enemy action in the last war. The church where they were married, which stands on Ludgate Hill above the Thames, was rebuilt after the Fire of London by Sir Christopher Wren. The church may have been chosen for the ceremony because it was within easy distance of the Strand, where Margaret lived with her father, and of the river, where Penn's boat would be moored. Ludgate meant the Curfew Gate of the city of London and was the first to be closed at night. It is possible that the newly weds did not return through Ludgate, but went eastwards to Tower Gardens and the navy quarters where they were only able to afford two rooms. The choice of a lecturer – that is, holder of a stipend for preaching, usually endowed by protestants who found the sermons of the beneficed clergy too anodyne, locates the marriage in its proper devotional context. Margaret and William made a radical protestant couple.

By the time of his marriage, young Penn was committed to the cause of parliament in the civil war. This did not necessarily imply republicanism: many volunteers for parliament, especially in the navy, embraced the old-fashioned constitutional notion of a mixed polity, in which king and parliament complemented and sustained each other. The tone of *The Seaman's Protestation* of 1642, explaining the navy's adherence to the parliamentary cause, probably represents Penn's thoughts at the time. Its constitutional doctrine was meagre, but it placed great emphasis on the defence of the Protestant settlement: 'We, who are always abroad,' it claimed

> can tell no government on earth is comparable to it; especially for keeping a crown upon a king's head . . . the continuation of which is, was and must necessarily be, by Parliaments . . . In vain it is for us to keep the narrow seas, if some go to lose the land . . . we mean the firm establishment of our Protestant religion . . . Your safety consists in ours; your churches, aye and houses too, would quickly fall to dust, should we let pass those who long to prey upon your lives and fortunes . . . And for confirmation we have all protested in this manner: I, *A.B.C.,* do protest before Almighty God, to maintain

with my dearest life and blood, the Protestant religion, to acknowledge Charles, by the Grace of God King, of England, Scotland and Ireland; to stand for the privileges of Parliament; utterly from my heart to abhor all popery. So help me God.

These sentiments were shared by Penn not only at the moment of the outbreak of civil war, but consistently throughout his life. When war polarised the parties, he always sought a solution that would keep the traditional elements of the constitution in balance, and the threats of popery and absolutism at bay. This gave him a reputation for trimming, along with others who served king, parliament, protectorate and restoration successively. In reality, however, it was the political context which changed, not Penn's allegiance to fixed principles. As his son later wrote, "Tis true he was actually engaged under both Parliament and King, his compass always steering him to eye a national concern and not domestic wars.'

Yet in the circumstances of the summer of 1642, service to parliament was a drastic step, especially for a young man newly embarked on a career of service under the crown and about to contract matrimony. Penn's father, moreover, at his distant consular post, did not waver in loyalty to his sovereign. The news of young William's marriage elicited from his father advice which was as prudent as politic: 'to leave the navy and resume the merchant life, confiding in a Levant voyage to eschew danger and build up a competence on which to maintain a household.' The son's famous reply might just as easily be ascribed, for its forthright words, its inherent self-righteousness, its inflexible idealism and its uncompromising recalcitrance, to the founder of Pennsylvania himself; indeed, the way this letter foreshadows the course of Penn's future relations with his own son seems almost uncanny:

No. Nor is the world at that pass with me as you may conceive. When I have spare (if at any time I have) 'tis well known to some how ready-handed I have been to the relief of others. Nor do I make proclamation thereof to you. But only to manifest my duty, of which I shall ever be careful. Nor do I serve the state in hope of gain. Gold to me, in this, is dirt. Tis the goodness of the cause that has only put me on and nothing whatsoever shall take me off from the service I have so cordially undertaken, and shall be so prodigal of my blood, that I shall think it well, very well spent, and life to boot, for the maintenance of so good, so just, so pious a quarrel. And if ever God send peace, an honourable peace, peace and truth on this our nation I may then, if I continue with the sea, think of a Levant voyage. Till then, though I spend more than I get (which is true enough), I am so resolved, and God so prosper my designs.

There is no reason to doubt the sincerity of Penn's pious claims. It remains true, however, that great advantage was to accrue to him from his decision to remain in naval service. One effect of the war was to exalt the fortunes of the professional navigators and experienced seamen in the navy. The Earl of Warwick – parliament's choice as Lord High Admiral – was a true sailor, who had indulged in piracy against the Spaniards in the Caribbean; his appointment, in preference to the king's placeman, Sir John Pennington, did much to engage naval sympathies on parliament's side. The most spectacular rise was that of Penn's staunch friend and colleague, Captain William Batten, to command the fleet in the Channel. Batten was popular with the navy on various counts. He had been connected with the service all his life; he had served as master of a royal ship for many years and in 1627 had been ordered to complete a survey of cordage at Chatham, he 'kissed His Majesty's hand for the Surveyor's place.' Therefore he was far from being the 'obscure fellow unknown to the navy' as described by that unreliable historian, Lord Clarendon.

Batten had a most pleasant personality and a kindly one. He was very merry, otherwise Penn would never have dared to write the bantering, risqué letters to him which he did when serving under him in the Irish guard; but then both men came from Bristol, a very strong bond. Under Warwick, Batten worked loyally to 'prevent the bringing over soldiers, money, ordinance from beyond the seas to assist the king against the Parliament of England'. The two houses had already sent a Remonstrance to the States of Holland in September 1642 to prevent them sending men, money and materials, to the king; but the Queen took shipping from Holland and arrived on the coast of Yorkshire, aided by her son-in-law, the Prince of Orange. It was in the course of duty that Batten was alleged to have fired on Her Majesty. The story grew that Batten tried to destroy her. In fact all that happened was that she and her ladies were showered with stones from a cannonball that landed on the river bank.

Penn's role and even his whereabouts in the early months of the war are obscure. Evidently, however, he was participating in what in time would prove to be one of the decisive actions of the war: the blockade of royalist England. The navy ringed the island of Great Britain, holding at bay the succour that might otherwise have sustained the royalist war effort. The ship Penn already commanded, the *Fellowship* of twenty-eight guns, had been confided to him soon after his marriage, when he was still only twenty-one years old. He could be equally sure of two consequences: rapid advancement and unavoidable envy. The pace of both was quickened on 12th April, 1644, when Penn was appointed to command the *Fellowship* in the Irish squadron. From this point, the chronicle of his deeds begins in earnest: it forms a case-study of the influence of sea-power on the course of the English revolution, demonstrating first how command of the seas decisively favoured parliament; then how moderate elements in the navy contributed to the Restoration and ensured its success.

For the immediate future, however, the importance of Penn's promotion was that it eased his circumstances. He and Margaret could now afford to move from their two small rooms to a house

'built with brick linings backward and adjoining to the east side of the former tenement, consisting of one hall and parlour and kitchen . . . with divided cellar underneath same and, above stairs, in first storey two fair chambers and on second storey two more and two garrets over the same with a yard before the same, now in the possession of William Penn.'

Strangely enough the house actually belonged to Charles I and in this house the future founder of Pennsylvania was born, on 14th October 1644.

It was during the month of July before the birth of Penn's son that news reached the committee of both kingdoms that the Earl of Inchiquin and Lord Broghill, with the Protestants of Munster 'intended to expel the popish part out of Youghall, Cork, Kinsale and Bandonbridge.' The Earl of Warwick ordered Penn, in the *Fellowship* in Irish water, to return to London 'to attend their pleasure regarding the prisoners they had taken.' Penn must have been overjoyed to complete his first voyage as her commander on this errand for it gave him time with his dear wife, who was now pregnant.

The other great news that month, however, was less welcome. Penn's home city of Bristol fell to Prince Rupert. When the civil war began, Bristol, whose citizens were almost wholly on the side of parliament, opened its gates to the parliamentary forces and built extensive fortifications, especially from Redcliffe Hill where the Penn family lived. But Bristol was far too important a port to be left by royalists in parliamentary hands. Charles' chief support lay in the south-west of England, and South Wales and Bristol blocked the passage of his forces for his planned attack on London. Prince Rupert was sent to capture it with 20,000 men. Bristol had only 2,300. The prince took full advantage of the situation and attacked. Blake, later the famous seaman whom the future Vice-Admiral Penn was to save at the battle of Portland, held off the attack until the royalist captain Washington, ancestor of the great American Washington, charged vigorously and the terrified horsemen of the defenders fled. Bristol was lost to Rupert on 25th July. His treaty with Bristol allowed the parliamentary soldiers to leave under arms and stated there would be no pillage. But the royalists behaved abominably. They robbed, sacked, burned homes and turned many owners out. How Penn's mother fared is not recorded, but as Mrs Giles Penn ended her days in Bristol and was buried in St Mary Redcliffe church, it is probable that in the absence of her husband in Morocco, and with her son away in the navy, her brother-in-law, the Bristol merchant, had her safely conveyed to her relations in Somerset until the troubles were over.

Penn must have returned on leave or naval services to London in the summer of 1644 for he was ordered to rejoin his squadron on 12th October. He did so, as the ship's log records, for the *Fellowship* sailed from Deptford about six o'clock in the morning. But this was only two days before his first son, Willliam, was born. In these circumstances Sir Harry Vane, one of the secretaries of the Admiralty, showed himself a true friend, because Penn stayed in the river another three weeks until 4th November, when the *Fellowship* weighed anchor and sailed to the Downs en route for Ireland. Before he sailed, the child who was to alter the course of American history, was christened William in the church of All Hallows, Barking, in Tower Street itself. So it was with a light heart that he met Vice-Admiral Batten and the Earl of Warwick in the Downs on the 7th November, where doubtless toasts were drunk to the proud father's son, under the cabin lantern.

Penn's first recorded assignment with the Irish Squadron came three months to the very day, on 4th February 1645, when he received orders at Spithead to transport Lord Broghill and a hundred of his men to

Kinsale. Lord Broghill was the Vice-President of the Province of Munster and Governor of Youghall, his home town in the County of Cork. Here his father had made his fortune and chosen the title of the first Earl of Cork.

Roger Boyle, Lord Broghill, came on board at three in the afternoon. He and Penn took an instant liking to each other. Born in the same year, travelled, sophisticated, intelligent, both had exercised big responsibilities for their years. Broghill's brother was Robert Boyle the philosopher, and he saw beyond the prejudices that accrue from one's upbringing. He recognised Penn for the great seaman and thinker that he was, despite his never having been to Oxford. Penn was a good host, quick-witted, entertaining, friendly and obviously loved by his men and officers. A warm friendship was formed which lasted to the end of Penn's life, and was continued through the second generation.

The ship's log reads: 'about two o'clock we came to an anchor in the harbour of Kinsale; and there my Lord and his men went ashore. God be praised for their safe arrival!' The responsibility for that pirate-infested crossing had been great indeed and Penn's relief was understandable. Even when he became accustomed to success, he was never blasé, and never omitted due tribute to Providence.

CHAPTER TWO

The Vice-Admiral

With the end of the campaigning season, the sources grow sparse. Penn resumed the routine work of the Irish guard. We hear of a ship captured and of intercepted papers from the king, at which the Earl of Warwick rejoiced. But at our next substantial news of Penn we find him anchored at Milford – the headquarters of the squadron – in early June, 1645, at a momentous junction of his career. Captain Richard Swanley, the commander of the Irish fleet, sent for Penn and said he intended to make the young captain his Vice-Admiral. On 3rd June Penn wrote

> The admiral gave me a warrant to go on board and take possession of the *Happy Entrance, Regis,* and so to be his vice-admiral, himself also going on board with me and making a speech to the company. I was joyfully received; and by general consent, accepted of, in the room and place of their deceased captain. The admiral then desired me to go on board our own ship the *Fellowship,* taking William Lawrence, his lieutenant, with me, declaring his and my desire, that seeing I was to leave them they would be pleased to accept the said Lawrence in my stead for their captain and commander. So I took my leave of them. At my departure she gave me fifteen guns; and so coming on board *Happy Entrance* she gave me nine for my welcome.

Penn was barely twenty-four years of age.

On the third day of his command the *Duncannon* had sailed in from Tenby with news that if ships were to be called away from Tenby the town would be in danger: the crew of the *Duncannon* had refused to go to sea. Penn dealt with the mutiny by persuasion. The need was explained to them and the men agreed to sail. The *Duncannon* then made for the province of Munster, to touch first at Youghall and find out how affairs were going with Lord Broghill, who was confronting the forces of the disaffected Irish, and then sail south-west round the coast to the harbour of Kinsale.

A fortnight later Penn found out for himself how Broghill was faring, for then the *Entrance* anchored in Cork Bay he met 'the Ladies Broghill, Broghill's widowed sister together with many other ladies of quality and the best of their household stuff.' Broghill had decided to evacuate the town before Penn should arrive and the battle grew hot. Reinforcements were needed and Lord Inchiquin, the President of Munster, 'with his own hand' wrote the orders for Penn to sail to Kinsale and there embark one hundred soldiers and transport them to Youghall. For Penn, however, it seems that the importance of these orders was eclipsed by a secret joy. Inchiquin might issue orders but his wife gave me a letter which she brought from mine.' This glorious fact was so important to Penn that it is the sole entry for the day, 26th June: not even the direction of the wind, nor its strength, which are customarily the first entries of each day. Unfortunately the previous letter, like all Margaret Penn's other letters, save one, has been lost. He received the letters seven months and thirteen days after taking leave of his beloved and their baby son. It was to be over thirteen months before he saw them again. A parting of some twenty-one months in all.

Penn now commanded three ships: his own *Happy Entrance* which was the eighth largest ship in the Irish fleet that summer, in a list of 62 vessels; the other two ships were the *Duncannon* and the *Nicholas*. As Penn prepared to sail, news reached them of the battle of Naseby, 'a great defeat the King had received'. Penn's ships were still riding in the harbour on Kinsale when a boat from Youghall sailed in with news that the soldiers beseiged there had sallied out twice and killed 300 of the enemy. This heartening news came as they waited for high tide to enable them to cross the sand bar which divides the land-locked harbour. That afternoon Penn anchored in the bay of Youghall and with his two other ships rode before the town'. Then a relation of Broghill's, Captain Boyle, came on board and invited him to dine with the Deputy Governor.

History was under the young Vice-Admiral's feet as he walked through the Water Gate up hill to the house called Myrtle Grove, once the home of Sir Walter Raleigh, now the home of the Boyle family where Sir Percy was living. The house stands just inside the fortified north wall of Youghall and immediately next to the church of St Mary Collegiate, which Henry VIII had given to Protestants at the time of the Reformation. Queen Elizabeth gave the house to Sir Walter Raleigh with forty thousand acres. Here was planted the first tobacco to be grown in the Old World. Here the first potatoes grew while Raleigh was Mayor of Youghall. At Myrtle Grove, Penn and the Deputy Governor, Sir Percy Smith, formulated their joint plan of action by naval reinforcement of the land forces and at five o'clock Sir Percy escorted the admiral back to his barge and saluted his departure with five guns. Penn returned the salute with three guns from the *Entrance.* But writing up his Log that evening, he noted with distress that 'at firing of the last gun of three, the piece not being well sponged, took fire as one of our men was ramming home the cartridge, and so unhappily blew off one of his hands'.

It was Penn's task to drive off, if not wipe out, the Catholic confederates surrounding the town whose inhabitants were starving. The Protestants tried gallantly to hold the Bay of Youghall while the whole of the interior was possessed by the enemy who could reinforce their fighters by sending ships down the Blackwater river into the harbour itself. The local Irish knew the channel; parliament's navy did not. But parliament desperately needed the port of Youghall to prevent overseas help reaching the Catholic confederation.

Penn had been asked not to anchor his ships in the harbour, but upstream in the Blackwater river, where, when the tide went down, the ships could get stuck. He did it most unwillingly but Sir Percy wanted one ship upstream to guard the town with his ships and 'the *Nicholas* to ride at the south end of the town, and the *Duncannon* at the north end, that they might play upon the enemy with their great guns, if the enemy should fall (as was much expected and feared) on either end of the town'.

At break of day on 17th July, Penn's worst fears were realised. Shore guns fired at the *Duncannon* and she blew up before his eyes and immediately sank. It happened because of an unexpected accident. The navy ships often carried wives and women on board. Though Penn never took his own wife into danger, he wisely made no attempt to stop the practice in his squadron. It seemed that just as a woman walked into the *Duncannon's* powder room, carrying a lit candle, a stray shot from the eastern shore blew her head off and the flaming candle dropped into a powder cask. It must have been one of the most effective shots in the civil war. There were eighteen deaths, plus casualties.

Later that day Penn went on shore to dine with the Governor when word came that two enemy boats were coming down river to bring

ammunition to the guns that they had already finished the *Duncannon.*
Penn ordered his barge to pursue them and then climbed to the top of
the town wall with the governor and two colonels and others. 'Taking
upon us to view the pursuit of the barge the enemy made a most
unhappy shot which killed the colonels and two soldiers . . . Five
others wounded . . . Only the deputy governor and myself escaped
unhurt, but with the stones thick about our ears, for which deliverance
God make me thankful!' After this Penn and Sir Percy retired into a
house nearby to clean themselves, and Penn wrote to Inchiquin asking
for replacement of the officers killed.

Inchiquin in turn wrote to the House of Lords giving, almost
verbatim, Penn's account of events, 'which greatly endangered Sir
Percy Smith, the deputy governor, in Broghill's absence and Captain
Penn, the vice-admiral, then but newly come on shore with munitions
which he furnished out of his ships's stores'. The letter explains that
'without these supplies by Captain Swanley, admiral, from Milford
Haven and by the vice-admiral Penn here the place would have been
reduced to the rebels'. Penn's Log continues:

> In the afternoon of the disaster, the *Duncannon's* men that were hurt
> were brought on board our ship. I have orders . . . to Captain
> Howett to endeavour the saving of sails and rigging as were not
> burnt; also that the gunner would get as many guns as he could come
> at, she heeling to port and her guns on the port side being all under
> water . . . I ordered that Captain Bray's carpenters should be
> assisting by cutting her gun ports wider that her guns might be easier
> gained. But the *Duncannon's* men answered that they had already lost
> all they had in her, and would not now hazard the loss of their lives
> also.

Realising the shattered morale of the men, Penn left the salvage
operation until the next day. But he would not admit defeat. The next
morning he sent the barge to the shore with some of his own sailors to
assist the *Duncannon's* crew to save what they could. They would not
help. So Penn personally got out the two best guns with the help of his
six best gunners. Under occasional fire in that narrow channel it was no
mean feat, for his own boat might have stuck fast like the *Duncannon.*

Penn's treatment of the *Duncannon's* feckless crew may seem
indulgent; it is more likely to have been merely prudent. For, when
occasion demanded, he could be a stern, even a harsh, disciplinarian. At

such times it became clear why he achieved his promotion at an age when other officers were only captains or less. On 5th August a bark arrived laden with provisions. Penn records in his log, 'The master of the bark, seeing how the enemy had blocked up the harbour, refused to go in. I told him what a shame this was but he refused. At last I told him his vessel *should* go in; and if he would not venture it willingly, he should be seized to the mast, and carried in whether he would or no.' Sensing the steel in the character of the young vice-admiral, the man finally consented to go in. Penn then helped him by putting eight navy men on board. Then, a nice additional touch, he gave his men half-a-crown to encourage them; an enormous sum in the seventeenth century!

Meanwhile, the state of stalemate in Youghall inspired him to another bold strategem. He ordered guns of salute to be fired on board each of his ships so that the garrison of the town would think reinforcements had arrived. *Happy Entrance* fired seven shots and *Nicholas* and *Mayflower,* which had replaced *Duncannon,* five apiece. The result was all Penn could have wished. The soldiers sallied out, captured some ordnance and threw it over the cliff; three hundred of the enemy were killed. Had Penn been in command on shore, the soldiers might have shown this sort of spirit from the beginning.

Such short-term strokes could not conclude the fight and Penn chaffed at his indecisive role as spectator of the siege. While the enemy was re-stocked with big guns by land, Penn did not have enough ammunition to make a bold attack. He pleaded to Swanley, 'Admiral and Sir, I have been industrious night and day. But now the enemy have blocked the harbour by great guns so that we cannot pass in or out to relieve the distressed place.' With ammunition he could land and drive the enemy away. He begged the admiral, 'if there be no supply from England, to order me one way or the other'.

Towards the middle of August, Penn got his reply: it did not, however, come from Swanley. That capable commander had been called from Milford to answer unfounded charges in London. Now the Admiralty sent the frigate *Charles* to Youghall, bringing Captain Crowther to take over from Penn, despite facts which proved Penn had been acting successfully all the time. It was a purely political decision such as has occurred from time to time in our history when politics have over-ruled the knowledge and experience of our fighting forces.

It was a great blow to Penn and his men were not inclined to accept the change of command willingly. On 18th August he reported, 'having heard muttering among the company, arising upon change of commanders; and fearing it might break forth into some mutinous disaster, I endeavoured by many persuasive arguments to allay it. Having pacified the most I caused the whole company to be assembled upon the deck, and freely delivered up my interest to Captain Crowther.' He could not know at the time that Admiral Batten, had been greatly displeased by the moves and had written to the Admiralty in defence of Penn and Swanley. Penn wrote at once to his fellow-sufferer:

'Honoured Sir, The best of my respects, together with my prayers for the evident manifestation of your zeal and integrity. I am sorry that *they can do nothing else but talk,* can talk so much to abuse the State, to whose service you have ever contributed your best endeavours . . . I am very short of time, myself here in Milford expecting my former charge . . . for the present, humbly craving to be, Sir,

Your ever devoted servant,

W. P.

Penn then wrote to the Admiralty, being anxious to clear himself of any charges of dereliction of duty in Irish waters. The last paragraph ends, 'I make no question, being once so happy as to wait upon this honourable committee, I shall be able to give satisfaction; *and shall then expect the guerdon due to real and unfeigned endeavours.'* There is something admirable in this. Penn was not afraid to stand up to the lords of the Admiralty nor to say that he expected to be properly rewarded for his achievements. The reward he intended, as he wrote earlier in the letter, was not to be paid in honours or wealth but in honouring the promise that he should return to command the *Fellowship* in the northern waters of the Irish Sea.

His letter had part of its effect, for three weeks later, on September 15th, Captain Lawrence brought the *Fellowship* in to Milford with instructions for Penn from Vice-Admiral Crowther that he should take possession of her. He was, however, to continue riding in the southern waters on duty, furnishing the army with stores, while on guard. This was not Penn's idea of naval service. The sailing of royalist forces to and from Scotland and Ireland offered far greater chances of combat. He told

Crowther he had been ordered by the Admiralty to go to the north of Ireland, but Crowther replied he had received no such instructions. Penn also wrote to Admiral Batten explaining the situation. '*I, not being inbred to lie in harbour, and much abhorring such, in my esteem an inefficient life,* humbly besought the honourable committee to send further order, whereby for the future I might manifest my former zeal and activity.'

Batten's letter back supplied further generous support, for in his reply Penn says 'Tis not small joy to read 'You could wishe me one of your expected fleet to be sent by my admiral'. I should conceive it none of the meanest happiness (rather than spin or indeed ravel away my time and provisions in a lazy kind of life, by keeping harbour.'

He continued to bombard everyone he knew with demands for more active service: witness his second letter to Secretary Jessop: 'If it be possible procure me some instructions for the manifestation of my loyalty to the public service for I grow weary of doing nothing.' He added a quick disclaimer: He had not been literally inept, 'but yet, *hoc aliquid nihil* in respect of my former activity.' He continued to write similar letters to Admiral Batten and Secretary Jessop, throughout the autumn of 1645, yet it seems he could not resist making short forays when time allowed. He does not record his successful capture of the *Bordeaux,* of Flushing, bound for Waterford, then an enemy port. It was illegal to trade with any port known not to be loyal. The captain of the *Bordeaux* 'gave his company "strong water" to prevent their revealing to Penn, who had seized the vessel, that they were bound for Waterford. He had incriminating papers which were 'fastened to a spike and thrown overboard by the Chirurgein." ' The deposition is headed *The examinacion of William Dighton merchant passenger in the Burdeau of Flushing of burthen 200 tuns, taken before Captain William Penn of the Assurance Friggatt 15th day of January 1646.* The prisoner took an oath that 'the Examinacion is in all things true and the skipper did give all the Companie strong-water seeing Captain Penn comeing in knoweing he was a Parliament shipp, and prayed them not to inform that he was bound to an enemies port Waterford.' This everyday event gives a representative glimpse of life in the Irish guard based on Milford.

Penn's confinement to Milford lasted until the end of January, 1646. But from time to time, Penn's training as a merchant was put to good use for the naval exchequer, buying and selling corn, making a profit for the government. Though he longed, for recreation as well as for the convenience of such business, to get out of his office and take a ride in the country, there was the problem of a horse. Horses were in very short supply, being commandeered by the forces, and in letters to friends Penn constantly enquired whether anyone could find him a horse to buy. He asks Laugharne, 'If you shall meet with a good horse for my turn, be pleased to buy him for me; and look what the price shall be, I shall thankfully repay it to yourself; and acknowledge it to be none of the meanest favours. Sir Arthur Loftus and his lady are returned to these parts, whom for want of a horse I have not yet seen.' As Lady Loftus, the sixth daughter of the first Earl of Cork, was the sister of Broghill and of the widowed Countess of Barrymore, whom he had first met at Kinsale when they arrived as refugees from Youghall, it was a real friendship based in the common bonds of wartime experiences, not mere social acquaintance.

The subject of a horse is pursued in letter after letter. To Loftus again: 'There are no musquets left, but pikes and pistols you can have at your pleasure . . . Sir, if my wits can procure me a horse, I shall not fail to wait upon you tomorrow . . . I drink you health in good claret and wish you well stored with it. I should then be a Turk at it indeed.' A few days later' 'I should much rejoice to see you, but I must be forced to ride upon a wooden horse, or else be forced to carry my own saddle. Sir Arthur Loftus and his lady are dispatched to Cork but have left their very good respects to you.'

As winter drew in, he wrote to Batten, addressing him as

Most honoured Sir and loving Master . . . My respective services to yourself and my good Mrs presented. Since Bristol is open, Prince Rupert having surrendered it to Sir Thomas Fairfax, I would have wished it my good fortune to wait upon you, . . . but they keep me here . . .'

P.S. 'Tis now grown cold, and 'tis thought a cup of sack would be seasonable. Now the Malaga orange-men are coming home, any of your men, by your order, might easily give me a quarter-cask. I should be very thankful and as thankfully repay.

It was cold indeed and one must hope that the cup of sack became available before the 24th January, 1646, for that was the date when he and Admiral Moulton sailed for Ireland. His prayers were answered, at last active service lay ahead. He embarked on his third voyage on his beloved *Fellowship*. But only as far as Cork: where he decided to change ships. For he was bound for the siege of Bunratty Castle on the river Limerick and the shallow waters of the Shannon, where conditions demanded a vessel of suitable draught.

They sailed into Cork harbour the next afternoon to discuss with Lord Broghill, vice-president of Munster, plans for their future campaign.

Ireland is divided into provinces which are sub-divided into counties. Ulster is the northern province, Munster forms the whole of the south-western area and includes the counties of Waterford, Cork, Limerick and Clare. The dangerous, jagged west coast often rises sheer from the Atlantic. Munster is therefore a very large area and has the important Atlantic coast bays, such as Bantry Bay, etc. but above all, the wide mouth of the River Shannon. This river, with its town of Limerick, was, and still is, of extreme importance to Ireland as being the outlet to the Atlantic for American trade, for Europe and the Far East. The Shannon is 240 miles long and is Ireland's principal river and the longest river in the British Isles. The whole area drained by the Shannon was principally peopled by Catholic Irish though the planters were in the main Protestant. The problem of winning Munster for the English parliament was therefore one of no small magnitude and though troops had to be conveyed and landed where necessary, much of the fighting would have to be naval. Preparations took several weeks; it was not till mid-February that Penn and his admiral reached Kinsale. Once there, Penn had the good fortune to be ordered to return to Cork on state business. He was given a horse and guard and told to ride there, which on horseback takes about three hours. He stayed two nights in Cork with Broghill and returned with his sailing orders, for the fleet.

Moulton ordered Penn to take command of the squadron; its destination: Bunratty, near the site of his wife's former estate, the most important of all Irish Commands at that date, for the capture of Bunratty Castle and its surrounding strongholds meant the control of Limerick. Nine miles upstream, Limerick was as important to the Irish confederates as Bristol was to England, and like Bristol, defended by a wide tidal estuary. Limerick came second only to Dublin in importance, just as Bristol was then second only to London as a wealthy trading port. Until the end of the eighteenth century it stood on what was, in Penn's day, a small island washed twice daily by the tide. It could be approached only across the marches. From this strong position, thrusting into the river, it commanded all the traffic by water to Limerick.

The name Bunratty means the bottom, or mouth, of the river Raitey, now called O'Garney. The island was situated at the right-angle junction of the Raitey with the Shannon and some thirty-seven miles from the Atlantic. As Penn's actions would perforce take place in the shallow waters of the Shannon, he chose to hoist his vice-admiral's flag on a small ship, the *Peter,* of 10 guns, the better to control operations upstream as well as down. He left the *Fellowship* to defend Cork, but took with him two larger ships, the *Antelope* of 36 guns, *Anne Percy* of 32 guns and several others. En route he captured Dingle Couch, where 'going with the Lieutenant-colonel McAdam on shore to command the seamen, landed and about three in the afternoon, they yielded up both town and castle.' It was good practice for what was to follow.

On 10th March Moulton and the fleet arrived; on the next day Moulton gave Penn the order to command all the frigates in the fleet and to dispose of all the soldiers and seamen. This included seven frigates, and a hoy and between six and seven hundred soldiers. So at three o'clock that afternoon Penn led the fleet up to Bunratty, which he reached about seven and sent a trumpeter to Lord Thomond with a letter from his admiral and Colonel McAdam. Thomond received the man kindly and said he was unwell, but would receive them the next day. Penn therefore landed his forces on an island near Bunratty for the night.

The Protestant Earl of Thomond, who owned the castle, was descended from the kings of Thomond, who for centuries claimed to rule all Ireland and fought to do so; but the marshes which divided north from south had prevented the Union of Ireland in prehistoric times. Now the earl had a big retinue outside the castle gates; marshals, stewards, cook and others. The earl and his family lived in great comfort in the topmost rooms built in the turrets. There were tapestries, arm chairs, carved chests and cupboards. The tapestries on the walls must have been magnificent, judging by the early sixteenth century ones hanging there today. The modern student is fortunate in that today Bunratty Castle can be seen in all its former glory, for it has been restored to what it was in the sixteenth and seventeenth century, by the great generosity of two distinguished men: Lord Gort and Lord Failte.

The Earl of Thomond, though technically a Protestant, had so far tried to remain neutral in the Civil War. He had, however, leaned towards the king, who could give no help. The pope sent Cardinal Rinuccini to try to win his favour, but Thomond played safe. However, when the Irish confederates failed to win him over, they ordered his tenants to pay him no rent. The position became intolerable and Thomond strongly considered offering his place to parliament.

So it came about that Penn, dressed in the full regalia of a rear-admiral, the ribboned tricorne hat, the ruffled necktie, the shoulder sash carrying the ornamental scabbard and sword, rode through the castle park to the drawbridge, accompanying his admiral to be received with all pomp and ceremony before being escorted to the top of the north-east tower of the earl's private apartments and there to dine with him and discuss, in guarded diplomatic terms, the reason for their coming and if possible move the earl to their wishes. The man Pepys unjustly dismissed as a 'common tarpaulin' was now an ambassador.

Penn, ambassador, honest seaman by profession, was no man's fool. He wrote, 'We found his lordship willing (as he said) in what he could comply with us, only he feared we were not a party considerable enough to undergo so great great a work. We promised to do our best; and God blessing us we doubted not of success.' Captain Giles' training of his son amongst merchants and courtiers alike was proving of value. Before dining with the earl, Penn had studied what today one would call a top secret report, sent in by a certain Sir Teague M'Mahon which gave detailed comments on the earl's whole countryside and followers, with observations as towards which side he might be expected to incline.

However, Penn's command began with bad luck. His own ship, the *Peter* was moored at Beth Road, lower down the estuary. But the local pilot had assured him that the little frigate could safely go up beyond Bunratty in the O'Garney river, as they would have no less than three-and-a-half fathoms at low water. They sailed to disaster. As Penn reported to Batten, they took the pilot on board but

> He, being ignorant of the channel, as impudent not to confess it, about five in the morning, caused our men to weigh, laid our ship upon the top of a ledge, where she lay with her bilge upon rocks six foot high. The tide being gone we went round about her, with which lying she beat in a piece of her plank . . . At her fleeting she so strained herself (the wind coming to gusty, stormy weather) that we verily expected her to have shattered all to pieces.

The ship broke and 'split some of the trunnels' or wooden pegs holding the ship's beams together. The whole structure was in danger. Penn shot guns to call for help, which came in the form of Captain Liston in the *Roebuck* and together the ships' companies removed about sixty tun of great rocks. That evening at six o'clock, Penn's ship floated again, but the pilot was dropped and Captain Liston piloted them up to Bunratty.

Ships were not his only problem. Women and children and aged men living in Bunratty had to be evacuated, partly because of shortage of food, but also to save them from the confederates lying round the castle. They were sent down river to sail with the Admiral's ships while Penn sent the *Antelope* a mile upstream to look out for any fireships coming from Limerick. Then he turned to the defence of Bunratty itself, calling the rest of his captains on board for consultation.

As well as the circle of earthworks and tidal marshland, the castle stood on high ground and had its own defence of a high earth mound. Penn decided to build this up and floor it so that guns could be mounted should occasion arise. The next plan was to attack the Irish at Sixmile Bridge. But they were forestalled. At five o'clock in the morning on 1st April, 120 horse and 300 foot arrived without being seen, using the cover of the woods and setting fire to houses in Bunratty; the thatched roofs made it easy. A party of twenty-five horse charged at them from the garrison and a shot badly wounded their leader, – Captain McGrath; panic then seized the Irish troops, who fled. Eighty of them were killed, a hundred taken prisoner including McGrath. No parliamentarian was hurt. Delighted with this success, Penn and McAdam rode out together at the head of fifty horse and 600 foot with light field guns and reached Sixmile Bridge that afternoon. The next morning they went back, fired the houses at Sixmile Bridge and captured 250 barrels of oatmeal, a great prize considering the shortage of provisions. When they returned with more prizes they found McGrath had died. He was given an honourable burial with three volleys of shot over his grave.

On Sunday, the 5th, 'there was no business but the duties of the day'. It is possible that one did not fight on that holy day, but the next morning Penn was out early strengthening his garrison. The huge stone pigeon house was converted into a gun emplacement and Bunratty garden wall was raised to form a breast work. Penn had to send his sailors to do this for the troops destined for his support were not forthcoming. They were delayed: as Crowther wrote to Speaker Lenthall, 'The contrary winds hinder me with twenty sail of merchantmen and Colonel Jefferson's horses going for Ireland. We are ready to set sail at first wind.'

Perhaps in this case the delay was fortunate, for food was scarce. Penn went from one island to another in the estuary in search of cattle. He found only a few horses and deer. News came that the rebels had carried off all the sheep and cattle that Penn had transported to the island of Enislow, which 'grieved me to hear, having taken such care of and transported to Enislow'. Some of the sailors and soldiers, 'ran away to the rogues'; but in defence of these defaulters, it must be said they fled inland where food was abundant.

At length on the 9th May, Lord Thomond embarked on a ship which was to sail to Cork, from where he could sail to England. As Penn had letters of importance to send to his admiral, he dispatched him 'away with all possible speed', having first given the earl full diplomatic treatment: a dinner on board, 'with five guns on his entering and when my lord took leave, nine guns'.

But the rebels were advancing. They took Cappah Castle two miles from Bunratty and though those within the castle resisted very gallantly, 'they yielded up for their lives'. Then the rebels marched to the castle of Rossmannahane only one mile from Bunratty, but the commander had quit and was now within Bunratty Castle. So this stronghold was delivered up without a shot fired. Penn was furious. He wrote, 'We believe the soldiers were hanged, as justly they deserve.'

Penn acted at once. Seeing the general want of ammunition he sent eighteen barrels of powder, shot, match, arms and other ammunition with Colonel McAdam's advice, appointing one of his own naval gunners for each. Then he sailed down again to his own ship.

The Irish confederates believed they were winning so on Sunday, 17th May, came a drum from the rebels demanding the castle, without any more ado as if it were no more but *Up and Ride*. I think their answer was as slight.

Penn was young and boyant. He was certain he could finish the job and despised the soldiers who had given up so easily. His answer to the Irish confederates alarmed them. They applied to the papal nuncio, Rinuccini, who at once supplied the necessary money for troops, – three thousand foot and horse – to be placed under the command of Lord

Muskerry. The nuncio was the man who had previously called on the Earl of Thomond to obtain his support for the Catholic cause without success. Now, in addition to the money for troops, he added the enormous sum of twenty-eight thousand crowns given by Cardinal Mazarin towards the royal cause. Muskerry felt strong. McAdam asked Penn for sailors to land and help him, for Muskerry was fortifying the high ground above Bunratty Castle. Penn went on shore to view operations and notes that the enemy on seeing him 'made two shot at me as I was with my boy in the outward works, but did no harm.'

It is this note which probably accounts for the statement on the only plaque on the wall of the Castle of Bunratty. It reads: ''The present O'Brien castle, built 1425, had undergone many alterations, but in the restoration works 1956/58 . . . the fifteenth century crenellations [were] restored. Admiral Penn was besieged here in 1646 and it is generally believed that his son, William Penn, Founder of Pennsylvania, then an infant, was at the castle.'

But 'my boy' was most probably his young cadet servant, as in the seventeenth Century men of importance had boys in constant attendance, who took the surname of their Master: witness Pepys, deciding to have a boy and call him Pepys, in order to copy the admiral.

If the infant William was indeed with him, he would have been under eighteen months old, which makess it unlikely that Penn would risk him in such an exposed position. It would also entirely alter the conception that Penn did not take his wife to sea with him in wartime. We know she was not taken to the Mediterranean, nor to Jamaica, nor on the Irish guard. But local belief in the child having been in Bunratty Castle is very strong because Penn's wife, born Margaret Jasper, grew up on her father's estate only a few miles from Bunratty, at a place still called Jasper's Bridge. This estate was close to that of the Dutchman, Van der Schuren, whom she had first married and it was of these two estates she had been dispossessed at the time of the uprising. Therefore it is natural for the Irish to think that she might have been happy to return to the region of her former home. Later, we know, she frequently went to Ireland and lived for long periods away from any fighting, on one or other of the Penn estates. But as other ladies' names occur in the ship's log, such as the frequently occurring Lady Broghill, it would seem odd to omit the name of the admiral's lady were she ever on board there or in the Castle.

The statement that 'Admiral Penn was beseiged here' is accurate, though misleading. Penn moved freely to and fro between his ship and the castle. He was never immured within its walls and when there was danger of women and children being starved out, he took prompt action to evacuate them. This was achieved on the 29th with difficulty, for the ships were themselves short of provisions, and Captain Smith refused to take any fugitives on board. Finally Captain Liston took them to Cork.

Penn now told Colonel McAdam to order all the ammunition he thought he might need. But the colonel delayed. Meanwhile Penn was so short of water for his men that he sent two ships, the *Roebuck* and the *Increase,* filled with empty barrels, all the way round the south west coast of Ireland to Kinsale 'for drink.' Beer kept for a longer period than did water, but drink was even more necessary than food.

At last the Irish leader, Muskerry, decided he must capture the little castle which Penn regarded as the key defence of Bunratty, for it much annoyed the 'Irish in their trenches.' But Muskerry failed. Then McAdam asked for seamen to be sent on shore to help in the battle, 'they being more skilful to unspike and break guns.' Penn sent some thirty or forty sailors to do this. He was asked for a sailor to command them in case they objected to being commanded by a soldier. A boatswain was therefore sent.

It was on 1st July that the tragedy occurred which marked the loss of the stronghold. Penn was summoned to an urgent council of war in the castle. During dinner the enemy began to fire at a fortified house adjoining the castle, which they had often tried to capture. As 'they shot so thick and plied their guns so hard' Colonel McAdam rose from the table and went to the house to encourage his men. He was inside it and passing a window when a shot passed through it and killed him, 'to the great lamentation of all.' He had been popular and was no coward.

The fighting never stopped. Penn went upstream to find to his horror that neither of the frigates, the *Green* nor the *Antelope* were there. 'I doubted all was not well.' It certainly was not. 'One had been shot through the hull and the other through the sail.' With the ships and their guns absent, the Irish had stormed the Little Castle and entered the garden of Bunratty itself.

The enemy leader, Muskerry, was a good soldier. He pressed on. The major who replaced the late McAdam was not the equal of his predecessor nor of Muskerry. The parliament troops panicked and 'made a confused retreat to the island where I found many of them at my landing.' Penn took command. He ordered the soldiers on to the ships and had them ferried to the east bank to keep open a line of retreat, for 'the enemy have enough men to eat us.' But despite further offers of help the soldiers swam their horses over the river and boarded Penn's ships.

There was nothing Penn could do except ship off all the women and children. Then he built breastworks and stayed on the island with his men until the tide was so high there was no danger of the enemy approaching even by swimming their horses. It was a brave last stand, for next morning a captain and a lieutenant of the parliamentary forces came on board the *Peter,* together with a captain of the rebels, saying they were compelled to yield. Penn demanded to see the terms and was told they now had less than 300 men, the rest killed or wounded, they asked quarter and to march to Cork by land, to quit the garrison with colours flying and musket bullets in their mouths, with artillery and horse, drums beating and colours flying. In this way honour would seem to be maintained. The wounded to be transported to Cork by ship.

On the Sunday morning all the ships came together in Beth Road, where Penns ship, the *Fellowship,* was riding. Penn went on board wet, weary and dejected, he sent for his commanders. Finally on 14th July the treaty was signed between Lord Muskerry and the Parliament's Major. Penn found the 'conditions so mean and so far beneath the honour of a soldier, that I should never have consented to. Yet, things past cure ought to be past care; and so I performed my part therein which is, to send up Captain Fitz-Gerald to the garrison with boats to bring off our seamen and soldiers.' He put the sick and wounded on one separate ship so that the 'whole and healthy might not be prejudiced by the intermixture.' They took on water and set sail out of the Shannon and into the Atlantic.

Two leagues out in the Atlantic they met a relief vessel with fifty soldiers on board and news that others were coming after them. It was too late. Bunratty was lost. It could not be stormed and re-won with the sick and weary, reinforced with fifty men and no rations. Penn decided to continue for Kinsale; but one ship, slower and damaged, remained very much eastern of all the fleet. Admiral Penn would not leave her to the mercy of the rebels. He ordered the fleet back again to where they were before. The rescue took several days, by which time 'the soldiers had drunk us dry'. Penn ordered every cask on every ship to be sent on shore and filled full; but the wind remained contrary; so next morning all the soldiers, women and children went on shore 'to pick, wash and refresh themselves, to avoid diseases which might grow amongst us; and so washed and cleaned our ships, the weather being hot and exalted by our infinite numbers on board, perilous.'

At one in the morning, as they turned to sail southward, the wind grew to gale force. The whole weight of the Atlantic rolled at them. The ships tossed in the very hard gale, with gusts of rain and a very great sea, so that we could not possibly weather the Blascoes'. It would have meant total shipwreck with the winds blowing the squadron on to the knife edge rocks of those small islands. There were two courses: either to turn back to the shelter of the river of Limerick, or risk the dangerous channel between the rocky shore of the island and the mainland. Penn could never stomach retreat. He chose the latter route despite the danger. However, only one ship dared follow his signal, and that was Captain Brown of the *Trial Pink,* a small vessel. By ten in the morning they were through the sound, but the rest of the fleet were out of sight. He hoped they had returned to the river of Limerick to await merchant shipping and sail back in convoy. It was what they had done. Ten days later they arrived in Kinsale bringing with them three prizes, the *Sampson,* the *Flushing* of Flushing and the *Salt Kettle* of Middleburgh, laden with tallow, hides and wool. It sweetened their late arrival. Moulton took care of the prizes.

These ten days of disquiet and the long discussions of battle plans had their effect on the sailor who had never yet complained of any illness. 'Being not well through the melancholicallness of the place where I had been mewed up, together with the sad success of our forces there, I was constrained to enter into a course of physic; and so was exempt from other business.' But the very next day Penn went on shore with the admiral to meet the lord president who had come to ask for help for the province. So the inference that Penn took to his bed in despair at Kinsale is wrong. Considering the responsibilities he had borne, which would not have been light for a man twice his age – he was still only twenty-five – and that the loss of lives and the sight of suffering always bore heavily on him, his conduct at Bunratty had been outstanding.

His first day of rest came on a Sunday, when there was no duty save 'the service of God.' A few days later, he sailed for England and at the end of four days, with a light heart, he saw the Lizard two leagues off. They passed a small fly boat of eight guns and fetched the master on board. He proved to be a merchant of London bound for Guinea. Penn set the master back on his own ship 'and so stood to southward.'

This ends the journal. From now until his next commission it was chiefly London which absorbed him – his wife and son and their house in Tower Gardens, his friends, Admiral and Lady Batten close by, and the powerful Sir Harry and Lady Vane. The Lady Vane, according to Pepys' story in later years, spent the time of Penn's absence in teaching Margaret Penn the manners and etiquette expected of an English lady. Knowing Penn's nature and love of joking, it is far from impossible that he teased her gently on her modish English behaviour and encouraged her gaiety while they romped together with their son.

CHAPTER THREE

Return to the South

When Penn broke the seals of his next commission, he found the terms changed from those to which he was accustomed. Hitherto, all such documents had been issued as from king and parliament, but on 5th October, 1646, the rule was altered and commissions were made in the name of parliament alone. The mixed policy in which Penn believed was falling into disuse: in the years to come, he would strive to save it from oblivion. He remained on balance of merits, on parliament's side, but his allegiance to a kingless state would never be wholly unequivocal.

If the terms of the new commission were uncongenial, its substance was highly satisfactory. Penn had long asked for a faster, new-built frigate and on 8th October this was granted. The committee of the admiralty met that Thursday, with ten others present, including Sir Henry Vane. Their report began:

'Whereas the *Assurance,* under the command of Captain William Penn, is ready to go to sea, and the approbation of the said Captain Penn thereunto is not yet passed the House of Commons . . . and for that the deferring of Captain Penn's commission will be a prejudice to the service, the committee thought fit to sign his commission; and the Earl of Warwick is desired to procure a message to be sent down to the house of peers to receive this committee's recommendation of the said Captain Penn to that command.

In the House of Commons on 10th October, the report from the Admiralty committee was read. 'And it is resolved that this House doth agree with the Lords; and doth approve of Captain William Penn to command the vessel lately built at Deptford called the *Assurance,* he having served Parliament formerly, several expeditions at sea, with courage and fidelity.'

To add to Penn's pleasure at his promotion to a new-built frigate of thirty guns, built by the Pett shipbuilding family, he learned that his former chief and friend, Captain Swanley, was once more his commander, recommended to both houses of parliament to be captain of the *Lion* and admiral of the Irish seas.

It was while Penn was 'seasonably preventing ships, going towards Ireland, that he captured a prize of unforseen importance.

'13th December, 1646, Sunday. About eight of the clock in the morning we spied a sail, to whom we gave chase. About eleven we came up with her and took her; she belonging to Waterford and was called the *Patrick* thereof, of burthen about sixty tuns, laden with hides, salmon and other commodities, bound for Bilboa; and had in her about eight Spaniards, passengers.'

This mention of his capture of Spanish prisoners hides a story of the greatest drama and tragedy which could befall any family. It concerned the sufferings of his brother George, the merchant in Spain, who had been in the hands of the Spanish Inquisition for three years, tortured all that time and still in solitary confinement in a dungeon. George was not the only English Protestant to be tortured, but he was Penn's only brother, whom as a small boy he had admired as his hero when with his mother he would go to the dockside in Bristol to meet George's ship. Therefore, the moment he learned that one of the Spaniards he had captured was Don Juan de Urbino, secretary of the Spanish viceroy of the Low Countries, Penn saw his chance to obtain his brother's release through diplomatic pressure. He succeeded by holding Don Juan de Urbino a virtual hostage. He humiliated the Spanish government and provoked public outcry. The case went exactly as Penn had intended it should. George Penn was released. A month later, on 12th January, 1647, the Spanish ambassador's agent appeared before an English naval committee to ask for Urbino's release. The report of that date reads:

'A Spanish gentleman, Don Juan de Urbino, being taken by Captain Penn on the coast of Munster in a prize that came out of Waterford, did this day attend the committee (together with Sr Bernardo) and desire that he might be set at liberty, he being a person of quality; and being demanded several questions by the committee, he alleged . . . that the ship wherein he was embarked was cast away about Waterford in Ireland at the end of June last. That he had embarked for Bilbao in the *St. Patrick* of Waterford, which was taken by Captain Penn, who did offer affronts to his person, stripping him naked and putting him among the common mariners; for which he desired satisfaction and reparation in his honour. And for that

Captain Crowther, vice-admiral of the Irish Squadron, informed the committee, that the examinations taken by Captain Swanley concerning this gentleman are in the hands of Captain Lawrence (without view thereof this Committee thought fit not to discharge him.)

Then on 14th January 'the examinations taken before Capt. Swanley concerning the Spanish gentleman, Juan de Urbino, were read; as there appeared no cause longer to detain him; ordered that he be delivered to mr Bernardo, agent to the Spanish ambassador.'

When one reads the Humble Remonstrance of George Penn, merchant, presented later to the Lord Protector Cromwell and compares it with Urbino's complaints at his treatment, one can only marvel at Penn's self-restraint. His brother's representations were attested on oath by twelve principal English merchants, factors at Seville and Sanlúcar and signed by them in London on Christmas Eve, 1647.

The affadavit records that George Penn, merchant, trading with Antwerp, had married a gentlewoman of Antwerp, a Roman Catholic; and lived with her many years in Spain at Seville, Málaga and Sanlúcar. They had no children so he brought her sisters to live with them. His great success as a merchant aroused the envy of the Catholic priests who accused him in 1643 of being a heretic and trying to seduce his wife and her sisters to the Protestant religion. His money, plate, goods and merchandise were seized to the value of £12,000 and confiscated. He was sent to Seville and kept in a dungeon for three years, and regularly tortured. He was tied to the bars of his dungeon when each month he received fifty lashes of a knotted rope. Then one Sunday, after the English government had protested he was led in procession and put on a scaffold where his accusers banished him from Spain. Then he was carried back to his dungeon, where at last light was allowed to penetrate and doctors and surgeons tried to set his joints and heal his wounds. It was two months and six days before he was capable of leaving. His marriage was annulled. He did not see his wife again. It was only at the end of 1647 that he was able to travel to London. He was a sick man for a long time. Later, the story was only just cheated of a happy ending. After the Restoration, to the joy of Admiral Penn, Charles II appointed George Penn to be his Resident Envoy to the Court of Spain. Unfortunately, George died at the Admiral's house shortly before he was due to sail to take up office.

One of the most obscure incidents of Penn's career was his sudden and brief fall from favour in 1648. The most favoured explanation is the most probable: Penn was suspected of complicity in naval disaffection and communication with the king. The background to the episode is well known. Throughout the summer of 1647, Cromwell and Ireton were negotiating with the defeated king, trying to impose a parliamentary monarchy: had the plan been given a chance it might have brought a just and early end to England's constitutional agonies. For months, messengers scurried up and down stream between Hampton Court, the king's gilded cage, and Putney, where the army had its headquarters in the Church of St Mary the Virgin. But the prospects were blighted by radical agitation and royal intransigeance. Agitators aroused and exposed the hostility prevalent in the army's ranks to any accommodation with monarchy. Charles, meanwhile, decided to escape. He picked his way secretly to the waterside and thence to the sea. The news was hurried to the Speaker who set in motion the order by parliament for the king's recapture. On 12th November, 1647, the order was despatched to Crowther and Penn: 'We pray and require you to stop and search all ships . . . in case you find on board his majesty's person, you are to make stay of him.'

In Penn's habitual circle, this turn of events was a severe test of loyalty to the parliamentary cause. The inexorable drift towards a republican form of government broke with the spirit of *the Seaman's Protestation* of 1643; many – perhaps most – of Penn's friends and comrades would probably have been satisfied with a constitutional compromise that strengthened and safeguarded the Protestant settlement. Henceforth, it was not uncommon for them to keep open their channels of communication to the royalist camp and look ahead to a time when a restoration on acceptable terms might be possible. One might call this a double game, if one will, but it was a way of maintaining, between divergent parties, fidelity to fixed principles. It was also a way of danger, to which Penn and some of his closest associates quickly proved to be vulnerable.

Captain Batten was the first to fall. The vice-admiral of the fleet was called before the committee on 14th September, 1647 'so that some matters objected against him may be imparted to him'. The reason was his own sympathy for the king and certain offers he had made to the royalists. Called before Sir Harry Vane and others he rendered up his commission. On 5th October the commissioners of the Navy received an order for payment to Captain Batten as vice admiral of the fleet for the summer's expedition the sum of forty shillings per diem . . . to that of being paid off.'.

The spring of 1648 brought the same dramatic change of fortune for Penn. Whitelock records:

March 4th, 1648. Three French ships taken by the Parliament's ship under Captain Penn . . . 1648, 13th April, Major Gray at the door brought intelligence from Ireland that Lord Inchiquin was revolted from Parliament to the rebels . . . Die Veneris 14th April ORDERED that Captain Penn be forthwith apprehended and brought up in safe custody.

No charge was ever brought against Penn, but his great friendship with Inchiquin was well known and suspicions as to Penn's loyalty to parliament were aroused. Penn was saved by the very acuity of the crisis in naval allegiance; the derogation of popular officers could only exacerbate mutinous inclinations. Men like Penn were needed: therefore they had to be trusted. Moreover, Penn's co-operation was vital if parliament was to quell unrest within the Irish squadron, where Penn's leadership was a decisive influence, and to induce the navy to accept Colonel Rainborow, Cromwell's nominee, to fill Batten's vacant place. Rainborow was a soldier, hateful to the sailors and representative of a drift back to the bad old ways, which had prevailed before the war, of using naval commands as a fund of political patronage. To the restiveness of sailors of royalist inclinations was added radical disaffection with the Earl of Warwick, who represented the old guard of moderate parliamentarians and was linked by ties of friendship or kin to prominent leaders on the royalist side. Naval schism and mutiny seemed imminent when, on 17th May, the day of Rainborow's appointment, Penn was released, and returned to his ship as rear-admiral of Ireland.

His treatment rankled – more, perhaps, with the navy at large than with Penn in particular. He got a handsome apology and the assurance of his political masters' confidence. From parliament's point of view, the ploy seems to have worked. Under Penn's guidance, the threats from the Irish guard were stilled. Only in one incident of great danger did the crisis erupt, when royalist ships appeared in the Thames and seamen who had deserted to the king sailed up to Chatham dockyard to make an attempt on Penn's old ship, the *Fellowship*. But Peter Pett, the shipbuilder, fought them off and sent the ship to Gillingham for safety. Then the royalists tried to seize the famous *Sovereign*. Pett armed a boat with musketeers and saved her. It was a commendable fight on the part of a man who was neither sailor nor soldier but a great naval architect. Had he done as much for a king, Peter Pett would have been knighted.

The execution of the king, a few months later, on 30th January 1649, has no place in naval history, except to say that no seaman was concerned in it.

In November, 1649, the Council of State wrote to General Blake with two alluring snippets: Portugal's Brazil fleet was returning home, and Prince Rupert of the Rhine, the king's cousin and commander, had escaped from Kinsale. Therefore, they had ordered Captain William Penn to be commander-in-chief of a squadron of eight ships to chase Rupert, now 'a German vagabond' in the Mediterranean. Blake had chased him to Majorca, but with provisions running low had decided to return. Cromwell was not too pleased, hence the choice of Penn to command the *Fairfax,* not yet ready for sea, but fitting out at Deptford.

Penn set sail from Spithead in the *Centurion* on 30th November with the first division of his fleet. On the 17th January Captain Lawson brought the *Fairfax* out to him, but the weather being so bad he and Lawson ran under the lee of the island of St Michael to exchange ships. When the crews and all the officers had been exchanged, Penn, as admiral, went last, waiting with practised eye for the boat below to rise on the water which must have soaked him with spray, as he too, jumped. By three in the afternoon the operation was completed. It had taken since five that morning.

In continuing bad weather, he sailed to the Rock of Lisbon where he found his instructions were to range as far as Gibraltar. The next day he met a convoy of English merchantmen and went on board the *Triumph* where Captain Hall gave him his latest orders: he was to follow Prince Rupert through the Straits. Penn called his captains to a council of war and decided the squadron should sail for Cadiz to tallow his ships and fill them with victuals.

Cadiz held bitter memories for Penn. It was where his brother George had lived for so long. Penn was no longer the young captain who had avenged him so diplomatically. He was Admiral of the English fleet. He sent a letter to the Governor of Cadiz and another to the

English Consul. The answer came quickly. Admiral Penn might freely make use of the port to tallow his fleet or make use of anything the place could provide. Then he was informed of ships that carried Frenchmen's goods. He detained two as he found at least fifty packets of linen on each.

In his letter to the Lord President of the Council of state – that is, Cromwell, – he enclosed a list 'of the ships and vessels, twelve in all, seized by Capt. William Penn, in this present expedition 1650, 1651.' This list records the first of many valuable captures while chasing Rupert. In July he got great bags of dollars and pieces of eight which totalled more than everything captured to date by Blake. When he was writing this report, Blake had reached England where the Commons voted him £1,000 for his great service. Penn deserved no less.

With Penn's letter to Cromwell was sent Captain Hall's report: 'Your fleets meeting here, *so soon after the departure of the other fleet,* is of no less admiration to other foreign kingdoms than Spain; who much admire your quickness in such strength and full supplies. So I believe in a short time the Spaniards will grow to respect us.'

On 29th March Penn and his fleet set sail from Cadiz for the Straits. That night they were in the 'narrow of the straits' mouth' and the next night off Málaga. Later they spoke with three Plymouth ships and two Flemings come from Alicante but they could give no news of Rupert. They anchored in Alicante Road to fill with water and get wine. The governor of Alicante came on board, but Penn did not go ashore. Penn – perhaps from fastidious Puritanism, perhaps from dedication to duty, perhaps from love of shipboard life – never once went ashore in the Mediterranean, though his men were given shore leave. Some of the sailors misbehaved; one had struck the master of the *Foresight,* who was acting as commander, the captain being ashore. For this,'the man was by a council of war condemned to die this morning at eight of clock.' But Penn, who hated the thought, had the man pardoned. Then he sailed for the Balearic Islands where he captured a great merchantman of Toulon, laden with sugars and cinnamon. Then he made for Majorca to land his French prisoners there. For obvious reasons he could not keep them on board. This was done, then later he met a convoy of English ships and sent the prize home with them. He got no news of Rupert, except to hear that the French king had given him three ships. 'But where he is gone nobody knows.'

So the chase continued day after day. His ships needed careening. His men needed bread and water. At Trepani Penn showed his iron resolve. He met with refusals. They would sell nothing and they could not have permission to land till they had orders from the viceroy who was away at Palermo. Angered at this, Penn sent for the governor and 'desired' him to meet him on the water in a boat. The governor dared do no other in face of the fleet and the English admiral's attitude. He met Penn in the boat and 'he promised that all the bakers in the town should be employed baking biscuits for us; this night we filled upwards of thirty tuns of water.'

But it was not only provisions that occupied his attention. He wanted to ransom English prisoners. At Algiers a bashaw who owned two galleys came on board and offered as much bread as Penn would buy. Penn sent him a present hoping to facilitate ransoming seven Englishmen he had that rowed in his galleys. 'He held them at such unreasonable rates that we had not the money to buy them, but he sent me one freely as a present to answer mine.' Then he met a frigate of Algiers, took her under command, freed one Englishman for sixty dollars and they presented another freely to him. Two days later they chased a sail to the eastward, but it was so calm that Penn had to send his boat to tow Captain Jordan and on their way call up all the ships' boats for that purpose. In this way they captured the *Francis* from Leghorn. The captain's chest had twenty-six great and small bags of dollars. Then upon strict examination of the master and purser of the *Francis,* Penn found there was more money hidden in the vessel. It was this great treasure chest which Penn's son William, was later to recall seeing opened on the quayside in London.

Six days later, Penn decided to sail to Messina by way of Malta, in order to clean his ships. He chose Messina, so famous for its dangerous straits, which he could not navigate, but he sailed into the port where his men went ashore to obtain meat at long last. But the main reason was the strong arguments of his commanders 'for our going somewhere to careen our frigates; one was, that whereas we were terrible to our enemies by reason of our sailing, we should now become ridiculous, daily experience teaching us, that our enemy's ships go better than we; and that without being clean, we can in no measure answer the ends whereunto we came.'

Penn's was the first English man of war to sail as far as Malta since the time of the crusades. The historian Hume was therefore in error when he wrote concerning Blake in the First Dutch War that he was the first to sail to Malta. Through mistakes such as these Penn's naval achievements were made to seem inferior to Blake's as one historian copied another.

As they approached Malta, Penn, through his telescope, could see the red sandstone cliffs rising steeply out of the blue sea, a natural fortress that nothing man-made could equal in the centuries-old battle between western powers and those of the Middle East. He decided to put his French prisoners there for safe-keeping. They went in the long-boat with a letter to the Grand Master of Malta, Paul Lascaria Castella. But Penn's men had to be paid and their provisions bought. He wrote to the Council of State punctually to pay them, while using for immediate needs the money from the sale of a prize, the *Spirit,* which could never have sailed to England. Then he struck a bargain for the *St Peter* prize with a merchant for 19,000 pieces of eight. It was consented to by Penn's commanders, 'who did admire the merchant would give so much for her.' But Penn had not lost his old ability in the merchant ways of ten years ago.

False information was the real reason for Penn's lack of success in finding Rupert. As he wrote to Lady Collingwood on 15th May, 'I have had labour and anxiety enough to wear any creature to a thread . . . since the French came into the Mediterranean I have been in constant pursuit of them, with little intelligence . . . and some I believe fabricated for the purpose of deception . . . It has made me almost crazy.' One day Penn saw several sails to leeward with Holland's flags. He sent his pinnace, with a master's mate to know what they were and enquire the news. That afternoon, he writes, 'he returned and informed me that they were states' men of war and that the admiral informed him that he met Prince Rupert with five ships and a prize off the Lizard the 30th June; with other *malignant* news.' This word malignant meant 'false and deceptious intelligence' and betrayed the Hollanders' hostility towards the English government; enmity was slowly building up through the continued trade rivalry between the two countries; from time to time it erupted into confrontations, which were to lead very shortly to the First Dutch War. Penn wrote to Admiral de Wildt and received a letter from him which certified his meeting Prince Rupert as before. Angry and not believing it, Penn fanned out his fleet with orders to meet at Málaga where he heard that Rupert had been ranging the coast near Cadiz. Such a report seemed nearer the truth. So four days later his fleet was at Gibraltar and he set them to ply the Straits.

Many years later, Admiral Penn's son, William Penn received a letter from Captain P. Gibson, which began:

Honoured Sir, Pursuant to your command for my giving your honour an account of what I remember of your late honoured father, Sir William Penn, is this . . . That he commanded a ship, the *Fairax* at Cadiz in 1650 . . . we sailed to Majorca, Sicily . . . and returned to Gibraltar about Michaelmas 1651, where we stayed cruising at least three months. By dividing the fleet into two parts, three ships in each division, the admiral and one division riding in old Gibraltar road, so as to be in the middle of the Straits or further towards the coast of Barbary, to look out for ships going into the Straits. Few ships went into the Straits but were spoken with, if friends, or taken if enemies.

All this was done during terrible Atlantic winter gales so that accidents were unavoidable, as Penn records. 'The foresail and mizzen were split and in the forenoon handing our main-topsail, one of our men fell (as we supposed) against the muzzle of a gun and never stirred hand or foot in the water as we could see; which made us not hoist out our boat to fetch him, it being very foul weather, and lost sight of him; the Lord grant it be a warning to us all and be prepared to meet our spiritual bridegroom, the Lord Jesus Christ.' This or a similar incident inspired these lines:

POEM WRITTEN BY THE ADMIRAL ON DEATH BY
DROWNING OF ONE OF HIS SAILORS
   The boisterous winds and raging seas
   Have tost me to and fro;
   But spite of these, by God's decrees,
   I harbour here below.
 In one of his letters to his son in Ireland he wrote:
   Where, safe at anchor I do ride
   With many of our fleet;
   In hope, one day, again to weigh
   GREAT ADMIRAL CHRIST to meet.''
The lines may be by Penn as they are not found anywhere else.

Admidst all this, men had to be fed. In order to buy beef for them, Penn had to send the governor of Tetuan a present of forty yards of satin and three sugar loaves. In return the governor allowed him to buy food and sent him a present of two horses. This delighted him, but what did not delight him was the first-hand account of Rupert's cruelty. The lieutenant of a captured ship told how Rupert had murdered the gunner of his ship because he was an Englishman. 'Rupert commanded the man's ears to be cut off . . . then caused his arms to be bound together and flung him overboard into the sea.'

Prince Rupert's cruelty was well known. Even Clarendon reports it, though without any condemnation: 'Prince Rupert had, with notable vigour and success, suppressed two or three mutinies (in the seceding fleet of 1648, in one of which he had been compelled to throw two or three seamen overboard by the strengh of his own arm.' But for all his cruelty he was not successful at sea. He was chased into Lisbon harbour and again chased round the Mediterranean and took refuge up the Adriatic. By the end of 1651 all his hatred and burning desire for revenge was concentrated against one man: Admiral Penn had slowly and methodically defeated his ships in battle and compelled him to flee with the remainder of his fleet into the open Atlantic. Penn records: 'November 26th . . . about nine I received a letter from Mr Hill at Cadiz, which informs me that the *Reformation* and the *Revenge* were sunk between the islands of St Michael [São Miguel] and Terceira; of which ship's company none were saved but Prince Rupert and none more, in the *Reformation's* pinnace.' Among those lost was Prince Rupert's brother, Prince Maurice. Rupert was destroyed. Penn, not Blake, had defeated him.

Before the end of December Penn decided to return to England. He had not captured Prince Rupert's person, but there was nothing more he could profitably do. 'January 19th 1652, About two in the morning we bore away for Cadiz . . . On 11th February we all weighted, viz myself, *Fairfax, Centurion, Adventure, Assurance, Renown, David* and the *Charity* of Amsterdam, taken by the *Phoenix* and Mr Madox, a Bristol man with eight guns.'' By 1st March he was passing the Tagus and saw six sail come out. He captured them all.

Three days later, in a stiff northerly gale, Penn started for home and on the sixteenth, 'about two afternoon we made the Lizard (praised be the Lord!)' The next morning by ten o'clock they were off Plymouth and Penn sent a packet ashore, to be posted to the Generals and Council of State. But the wind blew so hard from the south-east they could not continue up the Channel. About noon they bore back again to Falmouth, where they anchored at four o'clock. To his joy there he found Captain Ball with all the Dutch prizes, save one sunk at sea.

The log continues: 'March 18th, Thursday, 1652 . . . I went to Pendennis Castle; HAVING NOT PUT FOOT ON LAND SINCE MY DEPARTURE FROM THIS PLACE OUTWARD BOUND: WHICH WAS IN LAST DECEMBER WAS TWELVE MONTHS.' This was true, for as the logs noted he had held all his conferences with foreign authorities on the water; they had to come to him. Now he was on English soil, in the castle where he had dined with the Lady Waller on 17th December, 1650. He makes no mention of any such dinner this time. But he was homeward bound; his thoughts and longing were for his wife and his son William, now eight years old. The next morning Friday, the 19th, the wind changed to a stiff westerly gale and he set sail. By Sunday the wind changed once more so that Penn had to take the prizes into Spithead, 'where they arrived before the great eclipse of 29th March, called *Black Monday*, which came about nine in the morning. Stars came out. Birds took the roost; it was a day of obscurity, 'called the fearfullest eclipse, of the sun seen by mankind.' John Evelyn said that this celebrated eclipse which had been much threatened by the astrologers, had so exceedingly alarmed the nation that hardly anyone would work and none stirred out of their houses. The Council of State had announced its coming as a natural event. Penn took it very calmly. 'There fell a great fog . . . we lost our company . . . it continued thick till the next day, when it cleared we saw Beachy Head three leagues off, and though I fired guns and made a weft with my ensign, they that were ahead would not stay for us.' Then as admiral he had to gather the rest of the fleet together to secure his prizes and so 'on April last anchored in the Downs (Praised be the name of our heavenly father!) where I met the Right Hon. General Robert Blake.'

The news that Penn was on his way reached London by the ships which had gone ahead. It quickly reached Chigwell, where his son was at the Grammar School, and his wife at home. Together they went into London and as Penn sailed in they were on the quayside to meet him. In accordance with naval tradition they would be rowed out to his ship, the *Fairfax*, and taken on board to greet the admiral away from public gaze. But it can be safely assumed that in his eagerness to greet them, he would be waiting on deck to embrace them there before taking them to his private cabin. After that happy hour, it was duty once more, this time a pleasant duty, which to the end of his life the admiral's son never forgot. The large convoy of prize ships lay in the river, their sails swaying with the tide as their treasures were unloaded. The greatest sight of all was when the five great treasure chests, full of silver and gold were brought on deck from out of the *Fairfax's* hold. Young 'William recalled years later how his mother begged for just one of the curious coins, offering to pay for it with the equivalent value of gold from her own purse. But his father would not allow it. Penn's captains also begged that some part at least of the treasure 'might be distributed amongst them and if ever it be demanded, it shall be paid, or we will serve it out.' But no-one could shake the admiral in his resolve that he would hand every ounce intact to the government. When he had seen it safely delivered to the Treasury, then and only then, did Penn hand his wife and son into their waiting carriage.

As they drove along country lanes and through the forest to Chigwell, spring was bursting into leaf overhead; birds sang in the hedgerows and primroses adorned the banks. The admiral's chest of family presents was stowed behind the coachman and the pair of Tetuan horses trotted after, with their groom, content as their new owner himself to be on terra firma once more instead of the rising, falling, pitching, rolling decks of the *Fairfax* they had endured so long. As to Margaret Penn, one thought must have mastered her whole being. Her husband was safe at her side. Every jolt increased her gaiety and their mutual happiness, till at last their home was reached.

That night the sea was forgotten. Nine months later Peg Penn was born. She was christened Margaret.

CHAPTER FOUR

'Bloody Newes from Sea'

Penn did not have long at home with his family. On 24th March the Council wrote to Blake to order a survey of the ships 'now with Captain Penn', and of their fitness to be continued at sea for two or three months longer. On the 25th the Lord general Cromwell himself, was asked to go to Chatham to see 'what forwardness the ships there fitting had reached and to order a speedy hastening of them forth'.

The cause of this haste was the realisation that war with the Dutch could no longer be avoided. There were battles over herring fishing. England claimed the rights round her sea coasts, just as is claimed today in arbitrations with the Common Market. In October 1639 the Dutch had defeated the Spanish navy in the English Channel and were then supreme at sea, able to mock England's egregious claim to sovereign rights over her home waters. They introduced tea from China and coffee from Mocha. Their colonial development in the East Indies extended to Ceylon, Malacca and in 1651 when Penn was thirty they settled in the Cape of Good Hope. They also had settlements in the Caribbean. It was against this background that parliament passed the famous Navigation Act of 1651, based on a petition from 'the well affected masters and commanders of ships', which declared the Hollander had engrossed all the trade at sea; so that English trade was destroyed. Parliament adopted the suggestion of the master mariners and passed the act by which all English exports and imports be carried in English ships or else in the ships of the exporting countries. It was a tremendous blow to the Dutch carrying trade and the real *casus belli*. Economic interest, which divided the English from the Dutch proved stronger than the common ideologies, protestant and republican, which might have united them.

Cromwell had to have money for Vane remained adamant that the Navy be properly supplied. In March 1652 he attended the Admiralty committee and was responsible for the provision of guns for the whole fleet. In his desire for a powerful navy, Cromwell depended utterly on Vane. So thirty new frigates were ordered with the new three-decker design enabling them to carry more guns. Perhaps most astonishing of all in those strict Puritan days, Commissioner Pett requested that shipwrights be allowed to work on Sundays. Vane's most valuable attribute of all was his personal consultation with the commanders of the ships concerned and his strict supervision of work carried out in ports and dockyards. All this increasingly endeared him to Penn, whose personal supervision of work on all ships under his command was later to annoy Samuel Pepys.

The design of English and Dutch ships was very different. The Dutch coastline, its harbours and canals were shallow, so their ships were flatter bottomed and drew less water than the English, which qualification rendered them more capable of sailing among the shallows when chased by the enemy. The English in contrast were built of tougher wood, with sharper keels, which were less subject to splinters and fitter to 'dispute' with rough weather. Another point in their favour was that when, as was the custom, ships put grappling irons out to board each other and fight it out hand to hand, the taller English ships could see over the screens surrounding the decks intended to hide the soldiers on board. More important still, they could jump down on to the enemy's deck instead of climbing up their ropes to it. Which was what Penn would do when he jumped and led his men to hand-to-hand combat off Portland Bill.

Ships are nothing without good sailors. The Dutch had a world famous Commander in Admiral Tromp, who had spent his days at sea from the age of ten years, two years earlier than Penn. The English navy was commanded by soldiers to ensure the loyalty of the fleet to Cromwell. General Monck was an able soldier who knew how to fight in battle formation on land, but as a sailor he was totally ignorant. Blake's competence had been questionable. Cromwell now made the discovery that it was necessary to have a sailor, preferably of long-standing, at the head of the fleet, and he knew he had only one choice, namely Vice-Admiral Penn. So, on 19th May, 1652, parliament ordered that Penn be second-in-command to General Blake. Harry Vane addressed the letter to his friend, 'captain of the ship *Triumph*'.

Penn was still only thirty-one years of age, but he never lacked courage in addressing his elders and superiors. Within a fortnight of becoming Vice-Admiral of the Fleet on 2nd June, 1652, he wrote to Cromwell,

My lord, it is humbly conceived, that the State would be far better served, if, as formerly, they placed commanders in all the merchant-ships taken up; for, the commanders now being employed being all part-owners of their ships (and fearing some not so clearly conscientious as they should be), I do believe will not be so industrious in taking an enemy as other men; especially considering, that by engagement they not only waste their powder and shot, but are liable to receive damage in their masts, sails, rigging and hull . . .

In the paper I gave your excellency . . . we desired that lieutenants might be allowed and placed in all ships carrying a hundred men and fifty men; which I humbly make bold to remind you of, as a business of great advantage to the service.

Your excellency's most faithful humble servant

On board the TRIUMPH. W. P.

Despite the great naval reputation of the Dutch, the English had a number of advantages, their fewer ships were infinitely stronger in build and gunfire, the famous *Sovereign* had 100 guns, the *Resolution* under the Generals had 88, the *James* 66, and Lawson on the *George* commanded the Third Squadron with 58 guns. There were many ships with 60 and 50 guns. Against this Tromp's Flagship, the *Brederode* had 59 and no other Dutch ship approached this.

In large, Tromp's plans were to keep his main fleet in the North Sea to destroy the English fleet, while the English commanded Blake to intercept and seize the Dutch East-India fleet which was expected to return sometime between July and September. He was also ordered to stop the Dutch herring fleet in the North Sea.

On 29th November, 1652, Tromp appeared on the Goodwins with eighty men of war and ten fireships and found, as his intelligence had informed him, General Blake with only forty odd sail. The reason was that with the onset of winter the sea coal trade to Newcastle was extremely important to London and most likely to be attacked by the Dutch. Blake therefore divided his fleet into three. He sent twenty ships under Penn to convoy the colliers from Newcastle, and underestimating Tromp's boldness in plying off the Goodwins, he sent twelve to Plymouth and fifteen up the Thames for repairs.

That the coal trade was the priority was the opinion of the

Comissioners, who woke Sir Harry Vane at four a.m. They debated it till seven a.m. when a messenger was sent to Penn with instructions in general terms to secure or rescue the colliers. Vane disliked giving orders to ships at sea as 'a great hindrance in the speedy setting forth of the ships in service, which is the executive part of the navy wherewith we are entrusted'. He wanted to leave naval tactics to men on the spot. This revealed the character and vision of Sir Henry Vane and the essential difference between him and the lay politicians of all periods who, from a distance, over-rule the greater knowledge of experts on the spot with 'Whitehall knows best.' Such thinking linked him ever closer in friendship to Penn.

Blake made a mistake in sending twelve ships to Plymouth in addition to the twenty he had perforce to send north under Penn, but despite the deficiency of his forces he decided he could not be affronted a second time by Tromp, so chose to fight. He fought as a gallant soldier handling troops, ship fighting ship in individual combat and not in the manner of Penn, for Blake had not anticipated the revolutionary tactics which his subordinate was shortly to reveal.

The Dutch were triumphant and Tromp put a broom on his main-top to indicate he would sweep the English from the seas. The English riposte, however, matched the gesture with proof of equally dauntless morale. Songs appeared, as in the *Laughing Mercury of* 15th/22nd September, 1652.

> Now Neptune binds his curled brow
> His rolling bellows tumble
> > The Dutch do sink, the Lord knows how
> > Tarpaulins curse and grumble.
>
> Our navy brave, stout men of war
> That in the Channel ride
> > Will make those sons of pitch and tar
> > Full dearly rue their pride.

Blake himself showed a spirit of greatness after his debacle. He wrote to the Council of State, from the *Triumph* in the Downs and asked to be relieved of his command. The letter opened, 'I presume your honours do long for an account of what passed between us and the Dutch fleet;

and I hope you have hearts prepared to receive evil, as well as good, from the hands of God'. He then gave an account of the battle, mentioning ships by name, naturally with no mention of Penn. He asked for the fleet to be reinforced and then asked their honours to receive back his commission.

The Council ordered an enquiry but refused to take back Blake's commission. Then they wrote to General Monck and desired him to be ready to go to sea at twenty-four hours notice; he now joined General Blake and General Deane as one of the three admirals commanding the fleet. Monck was given command of the Third or White Squadron, which supported but did not lead the other two. Blake was restored to the First or Red Squadron together with Deane, supported by Lawson, while Penn was put in command of the Second or Blue Squadron. They did not have to wait many weeks for battle, because it was Tromp's chief duty to ply the Channel to meet the Dutch East India fleet on its homeward voyage and convoy it safely back to Holland. The most dangerous part of its voyage home was off Portland. For Portland Bill, being the nearest point to Cape de la Hague, was England's first and main defence against enemies coming up Channel from the Atlantic. Portland Bill is the extreme tip of an exceedingly dangerous coast, for any ship sailing eastward. The prevailing winds blow them towards the east coast of Lyme Bay, where from Abbotsbury to Portland the whole coast is protected by the famous, or infamous, Chesil Beach. This geological freak, an eight mile stretch of cliff made of pebbles whose size is strictly graded from great boulders at the mainland end, to infinitely small shingle at Portland, is of infinite danger to sailing ships. Pirates used to find their position by going near it to pick up a pebble. But in a strong west wind no sailing ship could get away from this graveyard. If ships failed to round the point of Portland Bill, then the even more deadly Portland Race, given an easterly wind proved to be their graveyard, for round that point seven currents meet over a mass of under-water islands. The navy of today tests escape and survival methods in that deadly race. Safe behind these hazards lie the harbours of Weymouth and Melcombe Regis which were to play an important part in Penn's life after the Restoration, when he became their member of parliament.

Tromp decided that he would not adhere to the former custom of putting his convoy of merchant ships in the safer waters of the mid-

English channel, instead he went as close to the English shore as he considered safe, putting his convoy between the coast and himself. He felt sure the English would expect him to take the normal, safer course in mid-channel. He had two hundred merchantmen with him and believed he had outwitted the English this time. But he had reckoned without Penn. Penn remained to windward ahead of the generals. Blake had with him some dozen ships when he saw Tromp. Lawson was astern where Blake could have joined him. But his weakness as commander showed once more, not the navy but his own reputation was at stake, he decided to fight rather than seem to give way. Tromp had the advantage of wind and numbers. Blake was soon in great trouble.

Penn saw what was happening and immediately sailed to Blake's rescue. He had long trained his captains to fight in line when he signalled them to follow him and not to advance in a drawn-out crescent as was used in the Armada. So, leading in the *Speaker*, Penn charged with his whole squadron following him in line, right through the centre of the Dutch, dividing their fleet into two. With the broadsides from his sixty-four guns, together with the guns of his ships behind him, he wreaked havoc on Dutch ship after Dutch ship on both sides of his squadron. The Dutch had no chance. Captain Robert Sanders, an eye-witness aboard the *Assurance* in Penn's division, relates what happened. 'General Monche, in the *Vanguard* and all his division being at least four miles to leeward of the other generals when the fight began' saw the outcome and did not forget it. Hence his recommendation of Penn when General Deane died.

At the time there was no doubt as to the name of the victor. Pamphlets describing the 'bloody newes from sea' were quickly put out and can be found in a collection of pamphlets 1652 and 1653 in the British Museum, such as *Another GREAT VICTORY obtained by Vice-Admiral Penn against the Hollanders.* Also *The Weekly Intelligencer* faithfully communicated affairs:

'Monday February 28th. Yesterday being Sunday, the ministers in the City of London and Westminster made in their prayers a thankful commemoration of the late mercies received in the famous victory. There is nothing more this day concerning Vice-Admiral Penn who hath done remarkable service . . . If you listen to the news on the Exchange they will tell you that Van Tromp is gone home with his as well distracted, as contracted numbers of merchantmen and his own men of war.

The following letter of 1st March 1653 from 'John Brown of Amsterdam' gives the most vivid picture of all.

Sir, The Ad. Van Tromp is come here with about six or seven ships, but so frightfully shattered that we can hardly distinguish them from Bottoms . . . such condition as would move a heart of adamant to pity . . . all the cabins besmeared with blood and broken limbs of men . . . Many Burgess and Merchants that were owners of those Prizes you have taken, are distracted, walking about the streets, their hands in their pockets . . . many of them broke.

De Witt has laid down his Commission for fear, or hatred of Van Tromp, who hath lost the victory and hazarded the whole navy . . . Amsterdam and with it all the riches they have been gathering. This is all I have to write at present

Your most humble devoted

John Brown

Typical rejoicing was reported by 'Mercurius Politicus', from the port of Bristol, which gave thanks for the victory as did the rest of England, and also took pride in a victory brought about by their own Admiral Penn. Compassion for men in trouble came naturally to that merchant city'. The reference to compassion was because the city collected £200 and gathered old linen for refreshing the poor wounded brought on shore.

To add to Penn's increasing fame, letters were received about this time 'that Prince Rupert, with three ships only, was come into Nantes; that he could give no account of his brother Maurice and his ships, which were separated from him by a hurricane in the West Indies and he believed they were cast away.'

Just over a month later Monck wrote to the Commissioners of the Admiralty, giving an account of an engagement between the Dutch and himself. 'One of the admirals was blown up, four more sunk, but it hath pleased the Lord to take away Major-General Deane, slain by a great shot . . . I have mentioned to Cromwell that Admiral Penn may be added to take up our number.' The commissioners and Cromwell approved whole-heartedly. So Penn became the first sailor ever to become a General-at-Sea.

Tromp could never forgive Penn for defeating him off Portland. As

English flagships, unlike Dutch, carried the Red, White or Blue Ensign on the main mast, it was easy for the enemy to pick out which Admiral they wished to fight. So when the English met the Dutch, Tromp sailed up to Penn and when he got close enough threw his grappling irons and there followed the most memorable incident of the war. It was recorded by Tromp's early Dutch biograpaher:

> Tromp grappled Admiral Penn, boarded him and poured many men into his ship; these being repulsed, Penn in his turn boarded Tromp . . . and his men were forced to fly all under deck. Upon which Tromp thought there was no remedy but to set fire to barrels of powder and blow up his deck of which the English were masters. In an instant the English were blown into the air, but this did not so much discourage them that they came on once more and charged him again; and being entered by Penn, he had certainly been lost had not de Witt and de Ruyter come up and disengaged him about seven o'clock in the evening.

Yet had it not been for the Dutch account, these facts would not be known to us. Praise for the action remained with Monck and Blake officially.

That great success was speedily followed by another of such commanding magnitude that it brought the Dutch War to an end: the famous battle of the Texel. On the morning of 29th July, the English fleet, having weighed anchor the night before from the Texel, sent its scouts ahead, who discovered the Dutch Fleet sailing with ninety-seven ships. The English gave chase, clearing decks, opening the gun ports, bringing up ammunition as they went. The battle went on till darkness separated the two fleets at nine o'clock. The next day the fight began again and the English hotly pursued the foe. The Dutch had nine flag-ships when the battle began. At last they had only one left, with Tromp's flag tied to the topmast. As it was shot down, 'Tromp's vice-admiral sank by his side' in the words of Violet Rowe, 'and the rest of the Dutch, much shattered, escaped into the river Texel.'

A letter from Monck was read in Parliament telling them that Tromp had been killed in the engagement. Amongst Penn's private papers is a 'Communication from Holland' dated 2nd August, which reads: 'Saturday, in the evening, de Witt lay at the mouth of the Texel and Tromp, sailing towards him, joined him that night. The next morning by seven o'clock Tromp was slain, being shot in the left pap with a musket shot from the ship that bore the White Colour.'

In this unassuming way, in his own diary, Penn reveals that it was his own ship, with the white flag, which got close enough to Tromp to kill him with a musket shot. 'Thus' says Colliber, 'ended the most vigorous war that ever was maintained at sea (for the war was wholly naval) . . . The Dutch Navy was completely shattered.'

Parliament did not wait for the peace treaty before they honoured the navy. Chains and medals of gold were given to Monck, Penn, Lawson and others. Silver medals likewise were distributed among the inferior officers and seamen. A day of thanksgiving was ordered, and a narrative of the fight read in churches. Then, on 6th August we read

> That it be humbly reported to parliament from the Council, that two gold chains, to the value of £300 a-piece, may be made, and given to General Blake and General Moncke, as a mark of favour from parliament and a token of their good acceptance of the eminent services performed by them against the Dutch; and that a chain to the value of £100 be made and given to Vice-Admiral Penn; and one of the same value to Rear Admiral Lawson.

A grand banquet was given at which Cromwell himself hung the chains of gold round the necks of Monck, Penn and Lawson and insisted they wore them for the rest of the evening. The scene in the Banqueting Hall at Westminster must have been magnificent. The dress uniforms of the men in brightly coloured coats rivalling the low cut satin gowns of the ladies whose dresses at that date were of outstanding beauty. There is no painting of Lady Penn in existence, yet she, like the beauties of the day would have worn a gown of satin, for had the admiral not given the Basha a roll of pink satin to encourage him to sell an English slave back to him? The delight of his son William, aged nine, at seeing his father's gold chain, becomes clear in the terms of his father's Will, in which he bequeathed all his jewels to his wife, a ring with a diamond and all his guns, swords and pistols to his younger son Richard, but to William the Quaker, who eschewed ornaments and arms, he left his gold medal and chain. The Admiral must have been conscious of his son's hero-worship, particularly as the family walked to Church at Chigwell to hear the narrative of the battle read as ordered.

Though the peace treaty was not actually signed until April 1654, the Dutch War was virtually over. There was no chance now of the Dutch being able to challenge the English command of the narrow seas. English naval supremacy in the Channel was at last restored since its sad decline following on the great victory of the Armada. But the Treaty was a fair one. Cromwell did not agree with those English who wanted harsh terms, and met the Dutch half-way. The provisions of the Navigation Act were maintained; the Dutch yielded the honour of the flag in the British Seas and the same honour from Land's End to the middle point of Staten in Norway. Penn was now in high favour with Cromwell and at one of the high peaks of fortunes. So he decided now was the time to ask Cromwell to make provision for his wife should he lose his life in the service of his country. Years previously as a young lieutenant, he had laid claim to an indemnity for the injuries sustained by his wife in the loss of her Irish Estates, which were not small. It was ignored. Now, as General-at-Sea, he could not be ignored. He appealed to Cromwell, who acted at once and passed an order in Council on 1st September, 1654.

> On consideration of the petition of General William Penn one of the admirals at sea; Ordered, by his Highness and the council, that as a mark of favour to him and in consideration of his sufferings in an estate of his wife's in Ireland, lands in Ireland yet undisposed of be set forth to him and his heirs of three hundred pounds per annum value, as the same were worth in the year 1640; and that, for empowering the Lord-Deputy and council to set forth the same accordingly, an ordinance be brought in.

To make doubly sure that Penn received his due, Cromwell himself addressed another letter to the Lord-Deputy and council in Ireland on 4th December as follows —

> Gentlemen, Ourselves and council having thought fit, in consideration of the great losses sustained by General Penn and his wife by the rebellion in Ireland, and as a remuneration of his good and faithful services performed to the Commonwealth to order that lands to the value of £300 a year, in Ireland as they were let in the year 1640, be settled on General Penn and his heirs; and for as much as he is now engaged in further service for the commonwealth in the present expedition by sea, and cannot himself look after the settling of the said estate, it is our will and pleasure, that lands of the said value be speedily surveyed and set forth in such place where there is a castle or convenient house for habitation upon them and near to some town or garrison, for the security and encouragement of such as he shall engage to plant and manure the same, and if it may be, such

67

lands as are already planted . . . We do earnestly and specially recommend the premises to your care, and remain,

your loving friend
[Signed] Oliver P.

The castle given was the Castle of Macroom, not far from Cork. No protector could be more handsome in his care for a subordinate; and no Lord Deputy would dare do otherwise than see the orders were carried out to the letter.

Penn was thirty years of age and second in command of a conquering navy. He awaited his next command with confidence although it meant leaving his beloved wife and family at Chigwell. He had chosen the village of Chigwell for a number of reasons. His wife's relations, the Jaspers, lived there and today one can still find a tombstone bearing the name of Jasper. The village had an excellent grammar school, famous today because William Penn attended it; it had been founded twenty years earlier and was built in two parts, which remain in excellent condition and are kept exactly as they were. One part was for reading, writing and arithmetic, with due attention paid to grammar, while the other part was 'The Latin School', where for a fee paid the boys proceeded to lessons in Latin. Penn had learned Latin at sea under his father, now his son learned it at Chigwell and continued with it under a tutor in Ireland.

Admiral Batten lived five miles away at Walthamstow, enjoying his famous garden of vines from which wine was made and drunk at Peg Penn's christening. In Chigwell is the fifteenth century Inn, most commodious and attractive still. Penn most probably frequented it with Admiral Batten, their jovial natures taking an interest in the lives of all men round them. The little village was not considered too far from London: a servant could be despatched on horseback to the pie shop in Fetter Lane to fetch a venison pasty, piping hot for dinner when company was expected.

The village was also distinguished for sport, particularly 'foot-racing', or racing on foot, before the fashion of football and cricket took over. The Penns were always athletes and blessed with strong physique, resistant to those fevers and fluxes which bore away countless thousands both at sea and on land in those plague years. When his father was at home, he taught William how to race, how best to start and especially to keep on regardless and never give up. It was what the Admiral had practised at sea; it was what the Red Indians in America came to admire in the white Englishman who so often beat them at their own games as well as in racing. William Penn later recalled his father's training in a racing metaphor, 'Though that has the heels, this has the wind and often wins the prize.'

CHAPTER FIVE

The Conquest of Jamaica

Military regimes feed poorly on a diet of peace. War with the Dutch had provided the essential conditions of Cromwell's self-elevation as Lord Protector. A triumphant peace confirmed him in power, but could not indefinitely prolong his dictatorship. Another war was needed – preferably, a religious war, a Protestant crusade, which would unite Englishmen at home and strike at potential fautors of royalism abroad. Ideally, such a war must be waged for profit. Expensive to maintain, because it relied on a professional army, Cromwell's government was committed to economy and low taxation – principles vital, during the civil war, to the making and maintenance of the anti-royalist cause. As Cromwell cast about for a suitable arena for English energies, there can have been little doubt where pickings were richest or where the prevailing ideology provoked, in protestant breasts, the greatest distaste. Since the days of Hakluyt, Walsingham and Gilbert, English protestant propaganda had called, almost without interruption, for the creation by war, of an English empire, at His Catholic Majesty's expense, among the rich islands of the Spanish Main. Under cover of the Thirty Years' War, English, Dutch and French adventurers had succeeded in cutting out a number of the smaller islands and wresting them from Spanish rule. Now, with the Spanish monarchy weakened by defeats and internal rebellions, and locked in a major continental struggle with France, the time seemed propitious for a new and concerted attack, a 'western design' aimed at the seizure of one or more of the bigger and richer Spanish colonies. The precise objective of the intended expedition is unclear. But some of those involved in the planning and leadership – perhaps, indeed, Cromwell himself – evidently meant to attack Hispaniola, Christendom's oldest New World colony and the jewel of the Spanish Antilles. Even in Spain's debilitated condition, this remained one of the toughest fibres in the King of Spain's beard. The extent of Spanish domination in the

Caribbean, the paucity and vulnerability of English outposts, were probably little understood in England. The capture of Hispaniola would have represented the equivalent, in daring and difficulty, of the plan in the last war to seize the Normandy beaches while the rest of Europe remained in enemy hands.

To engage in a war with Spain, Cromwell had to find an excuse. He sent for the Spanish ambassador in August 1654 and told him that their mutual friendship depended upon all Englishmen being granted liberty of conscience in all Spanish dominions. Considering how George Penn had been tortured (to take only one example) the question was not exactly an academic one. He also asked that Englishmen should have freedom to trade in the West Indies. The ambassador replied, 'To ask for these concessions is to demand my master's two eyes'. Cromwell was courteous and made no declaration of war. He held the ambivalent idea that war with Spain across the Atlantic might not mean war with Spain in home waters. So he pressed on with preparations of the fleet.

Cromwell had already chosen three commissioners besides Penn and Venables. They were Edward Winslow, Daniel Searle and Gregory Butler. Winslow was the oldest, being sixty-three when he sailed with Penn and by far the most experienced in colonial matters of the Americas and the Indies.

Cromwell had no difficulty in choosing the commander-in-chief of the fleet. Penn had no possible rival. To lead the land forces, however, Venables was chosen more by chance. The commission which Cromwell gave to Penn read:

Oliver, Lord Protector of the Commonwealth of England, Ireland, Scotland and the dominions thereunto belonging, to General Penn, Commander-in-Chief of the fleet and sea-forces designed and set forth for the parts of America, greeting; We, having taken into consideration the cruelties and inhuman practices of the king of Spain exercised in America, with advice of our council, prepared a fleet of ships of war, with a convenient number of ships burden to carry provisions, and to transport a land-army and forces under the conduct and command of General Venables, into America, to assult the said King of Spain and his subjects there; and it being necessary that the said fleet should be put under the command of a faithful, experienced person, and reposing confidence in the abilities, faithfulness and good affection of you, General William Penn, we have appointed you and do by these presents constitute you to be general and commander-in-chief of the said fleet and ships . . . Witness ourselves at Westminster, 9th October, 1654.

More detailed instructions came by hand of Cromwell's secretary, John Thurloe:

> Whereas we have made and constituted you general and commander-in-chief of the fleet designed and prepared for America, you are to take into your charge, the *Swiftsure, Paragon, Torrington* etc. Besides the said fleet, we have caused to be raised levied, here in England, land forces both horse and foot, five regiments of foot and sixty horse, to be transported under the conduct of General Venables and have appointed them to march to Portsmouth to go aboard there. You shall use your best endeavours to seize upon, surprise and take all vessels whatsoever belonging to the king of Spain. You are hereby required to take aboard such of the said forces as are ready, to sail forthwith to the island of Barbadoes.

John Thurloe

Instructions were given to General Venables that he should 'Immediately upon receipt of these instructions repair, with the forces aforesaid to Portsmouth, where he have appointed the fleet designed for the afforesaid service, under the command of General Penn, to take you with the army and land forces, on board and to transport you unto the parts aforesaid.'

General Robert Venables was made commander of the land forces because he happened to be on the spot during discussions, at the end of the Dutch war, about what was to be done with the land forces. Unemployed men meant discontent and he had arrived to put the case for his fellow officers. Ten years older than Penn, he had joined the parliament army in the civil war, become governor of Liverpool, had fought in Ireland, but never held supreme command. He was a widower, but a few months before the Expedition sailed, he married a young wife, Elizabeth, the widow of Samuel Alderney. To this marriage must be attributed a large part of Venables' misfortunes. He refused to sail without her. He was much in love. Penn, too, was much in love, but he would never take his wife to sea. He knew only too well the terrible misfortunes which could beset a woman at sea.

Penn was quite unaware of Venables' jealousy of himself, which had been expressed in a letter to Cromwell. Unfortunately, what had not been made absolutely clear was which general – General Penn or General Venables – was to have supreme command of the expedition. The fact that Venables was named first in the preamble to the commission created some prejudice in his favour, but Penn was named first both in the body of the document and in the instructions to the commissioners. Such ambiguity might have been calculated to arouse dissent. Venables, moreover, was outraged by that passage in the commission to General Penn which read, 'It being necessary that the said fleet of ships be put under the command of a faithful and experienced person, and reposing confidence in the abilities, faithfulness and good affection of you, General Penn, . . . we do give you full power and authority to order and command the same.'

The instructions to General Venables did not contain any such warm-hearted phrase. He therefore complained to Cromwell about the powers 'of the other Commissioners' and moved the resolution 'that my friends should not be made more formidable to me than my enemies, by bounding me with instructions which at that distance would but serve as fetters.' To which Cromwell merely replied 'You have your full commission and powers.' He seems to have thought that modified favour was a source of encouragement.

Cromwell addressed Penn before he sailed with a similar mixture of threats and promises: 'I hope that the Lord will have an eye on this business and be able to overcome everything in a man's heart that may be an impediment . . . and in this I have full assurance of you, notwithstanding some knowledge of a little dissatisfaction with you, which I hope by this time will be removed.' The Protector, we may infer, felt 'assured' of Penn's naval prowess, 'dissatisfied' with his political posture. Indeed, according to Clarendon, Penn was now actively contemplating desertion to the royalist cause, but was advised by the king's agents to await a more favourable time.

Cromwell's choice of the beloved, elderly planter Winslow was a wise one. He acted as a father to the commissioners and generals. Before they sailed he wrote to Cromwell that 'the sore was cured between the two generals', as if by his own healing balm. Unhappily, as things turned out, the judgement was premature and the cure incomplete.

As Commander-in-Chief, Penn led his squadron in the *Swiftsure,* the finest ship in the navy. Vice-Admiral Lawson's squadron had twelve ships and rear admiral Dakins squadron, twelve ships and one fire-ship.

This meant a total of thirty-eight ships to be victualled, watered and prepared for battle with powder, shot and all necessaries. This was a formidable task for which Cromwell's brother-in-law, General Disbrowe, who had been put in charge as victualler and supplier of ammunition, was totally unfit.

An excellent sea-regiment was formed by Penn's orders and commanded by Vice-Admiral Goodson, a sailor who had distinguished himself in the late Dutch War. But neither trained sailors nor raw soldiers could fight without ammunition or food and water. On 6th November, 1654, Penn wrote to the commissioners of the Admiralty, 'Gentlemen, I have but little news. Our chief work at present is to reduce the business of victualling into a better method; I could earnestly wish you would give order that 300 tuns of beer be speedily brought us, much of that here having proved defective.'

On 6th December he wrote again' 'Gentlemen, Holding it of great importance to the service in hand that we have along with us a very good load-stone to touch the needles of our compass withal (many of them not being very good) I therefore desire you to buy a right special good one, and send it speedily down.'

As the fleet got ready to depart, the inadequacy of the preparations increased the mutual apprehension of the commanders. Winslow, reporting their exacerbated rivalries to Secretary Thurloe, was inclined to blame Penn:

'Rt Honourable Sir, when I wrote to you from Portsmouth I told you how easily that sore was cured between Venables and Penn, whose demeanour, mutually towards each other at sea was sweet and hopeful; but the last of these two gentlemen is to apt to be taken withsuch conceits . . . Only I fear, that going hence without our stores, some occasion will arise of disturbance between land and sea forces.

A journal, or Ship's log of every day's proceedings was kept under General Penn on the *Swiftsure,* it was mostly written up by his secretary W. B., or William Burrows, later chief clerk of Sir William Penn. There is a second short manuscript also by W. B. but he wrote it in very small copperplate when dealing with private matters or those of special interest. 'Mr. Winslow came on board; understood Gen. V. and wife still on board.'

Penn kept his wife with him until the last possible moment. They travelled together as far as Portsmouth. It is to be believed that she went on board to say farewell in the privacy of his cabin; but when she returned on shore she left Mrs Venables on board with General Disbrowe and General Venables. Penn had already charged Disbrowe with the task of escorting his wife safely back to London and must have handed him a farewell letter to her when 'having taken leave of Gen. Disbrowe we set sail from Spithead, but the wind fresh at east we came again to anchor . . . ' So many Penn family papers have been lost that Margaret Penn's letter written in reply to her husband on 2nd January, 1655, is of special interest: 'I received your letter by our honoured friend General Disbrowe, who saw me safe to Kingston, where we dined together; and everyone returned to their homes. The two coachmen talking together, the while one of the wheels raised up against a bank and overturned us; but no hurt (thanks be to the Lord) it being a very plain way; it was hard by Godalming.' This letter reached Penn by one of the supply ships sailing after the fleet.

It is noticeable that though the fleet sailed on Monday, 25th December, there is no mention in the ship's log that this was Christmas Day: the Puritans frowned on the festivities as popish and evil. The following day is noted only as 26th Tuesday. 'Weighed again, but the wind blew hard at east and the leeward ships could not get out at St Ellens, the *Portland* was sent out with orders for them all what to do in case of separation; the place intended was Barbadoes; . . . Admiral Penn therewith gave commission to take or sink etc all ships belonging to the Turks (Algiers excepted), French and *Beyond the tropic of Cancer* Spanish. This instruction was Cromwell's artifice, to conceal from Spain his intended hostility until he should have time to strike his blow in the West Indies.

The Log of the *Swiftsure* continues. 'January 29th, 1655 Monday. This day in the morning about eight, we saw the island of Barbadoes right a-head. At three, we came to anchor in Hawkes Bay.' Henry Whistler, sailing-master of *Swiftsure*, reports on the next day: '30th Day . . . This day our general and General Venables and Commissioner Winslow went ashore where they were received with much servility . . . and it was agreed and commissions granted to raise soulogers [soldiers] by ye commanders.'

But despite the civility with which they were received they did not meet with the help they had been led to expect. Most of the settlers and planters were royalists or adventurers eager to seek their fortunes. By 1655 they had settled down and become traders, and resented Cromwell's policy that men should be taken to fight the Spanish. The log continues, 'The gentlemen . . . seemed displeased with such as had given an assurance of recruiting great forces . . . so they withdrew to consult.'

The recruiting of men was carried out by Venables with 'a high hand'. Venables issued a proclamation, by beat of drum, that any bond-servant who joined up should have his freedom. 'The result', wrote S. A. G. Taylor in *Western Design,* was that hundreds joined up and the planters lost a large part of their labour force.'

The fleet stayed at Barbados until 31st March. During those two months Penn showed himself very much the father of the future Quaker. His instructions to his men were animated by puritanical zeal:

BY THE GENERAL OF THE FLEET
AGAINST THE SEAMEN'S DOING ANY INJURY TO PLANTERS

'Forasmuch as I have been informed that seamen . . . under pretence of going on shore to collect water, have gone into the plantations and made spoil of the sugar cane and provisions, to the great prejudice of the inhabitants; these are to straitly command all seamen that they wander not into any plantations . . .

Given on board the State's ship *Swiftsure,* 1st Feb. 1655 W. P.'

Penn also made an order against profanation of the Lord's Day. No boat was to sail unless upon necessary business. Another order was for 'Captains to walk the rounds on shore every night.' No man was to be on shore at night after the gun was discharged and the watch set . . . If seamen were found tippling they had to be brought on board and punished.

Barbados was the headquarters of the western design and Whistler describes it as 'One of the richest spots of ground in the world . . . rich soil . . . grain, fruit, coffee . . . pleasant fruit as pineapples . . .' Then comes the appalling accusation: 'This island is the Dunghill whereon England doth cast her rubbish . . . Roges and hors (whores) . . . a whore if brought here, if handsome, makes a rich planter's wife . . .'

Before deciding where to make the attack on the Spaniard, Penn sailed round the little islands which form a semi-circle from the mainland near the Port of Spain to Puerto Rico. His reconnaissance done, he sailed back to Barbados. As the store ships had not arrived, a council of war attended by senior officers of the army, met to consider the 'wants of the army'. They needed 600 pikes, 20 half-pikes and more. All the local blacksmiths were ordered to make heads for the half-pikes which were fastened on to shafts ten feet long and called cabbage stalks.

Venables has been accused of wasting so much time in Barbados that the best campaigning weather was over before he sailed. His delay gave the Spaniards time to be on the alert. This was the accusation made in London at the enquiry which followed Venables' return. Taylor is convinced that 'Venables must bear a large part of the blame for the disasters that followed'.

Worse disaster would have followed had not Penn raised a sea-regiment under Colonel William Goodson. Penn wrote to Cromwell on 17th March, 'We have a very gallant regiment, consisting of 1200 proper stout seamen, who are headed by their own officers and exercised on shore almost every day. They are ready for land service when they shall be commanded thereunto.'

Henry Whistler records the moment of the announcement of the fateful decision to assail Hispaniola: '9th Day. This day all the land officers were called on board for councell. The general did declare to them HISPANIOLA was the place resolved upon and that Riuorhina was the place of landing.' The fleet sailed from Barbados for Hispaniola on the 31st March and the last note on the log of the *Swiftsure* before it sailed, reads, '31st Saturday. The general and his lady came on board and the governor and his, and many chiefs of the island and dined . . . After business was dispatched and letters written for England to the commissioners of the Admiralty and General Disbrowe, we set sail.'

The operative and tragic phrase in the log is 'The *General and his lady* came on board'. For when the farewell dinner was over, General Venables and his wife stayed on board the *Swiftsure* and sailed with the expedition. The presence of Mrs Venables was to increase her husband's natural cowardice and the attraction of her person and their mutual concern for their health served to devitalise him. This taken in conjunction with the comparative comfort of life on board as against soldiering through unknown jungles or leading his men in an attack on the fort, made him hesitate, find excuses to linger near the shore and the ship, saying it was wisdom. All of which caused tremendous discontent amongst his soldiers. The commissioners Winslow and Butler condemned him. It was Penn who took the lead.

Log of the *Swiftsure*, 13th April: 'We came in sight of San Domingo
. . . which lieth in a bay . . . the southern shores were low but rocky,
there was great surf of sea against it . . . so that the beating of the water
appeared for off like the smoke of ordinance.' The dangerous coral reefs
are not mentioned, probably W. B. did not know about them. But the
whole area abounds in banks and shoals. Boats could be easily
overturned in the pounding surf.

At an agreed place the fleet divided into two. Penn remained on his
flagship. Venables and his wife transferred to the Vice-Admiral's ship
which carried Colonel Goodson and 300 men of the sea-regiment (or
marines) and a great part of the army. They sailed to a landing place to
the leeward ten leagues from the town of Santo Domingo. As they
sailed westward Venables protested to Colonel Goodson they were
going too far west. He replied he could not approach the shore any
further for fear of running aground. He could not risk his boats in the
strong current and high wind, and they were carried helplessly past the
appointed landing place, before they could find a safe spot.

The navy quickly and efficiently landed Venables' army at Point
Niaso. They were unopposed. The few foe who saw them ran off. The
column marched eastward, led by the Reformado company, followed
by Venables regiment and others, the sea-regiment in the van. But after
four miles marching they halted and waited till next morning after
prayers before Venables moved on, by which time the enemy had fired
the savannas. The fires increased the terrible tropical heat and numbers
of men dropped dead for want to a drink of water.

The sailing master's account reads:

13th Day. Close in shore of Hispaniola. Now when we were in sight
of the enemy and all ready to go ashore Gen. Venables called his
commanders on board to further counsell them: a very unseasonable
time for it was time for them to be landing the army . . . 14th. Sailors
landed, remained in good order, none to molest them. Sabbath Day.
Army marched 12 miles . . . met plantattions but all fled except a few
Spaniards eaten out with smallpox. Sea regiment heard soldiers say 'Shall
we risk our lives for nothing?' The friars had gone . . . Soldiers found
rich plate and a figure of the Virgin . . . They threw oranges at her and
deformed her for she had Christ in her arms. But [with] heat and want
of water, many did die. Our fleet did keep under sail before the jetty as
soldiers would have run into the harbour they were to march from.

Penn had left the *Swiftsure* when the troops were changing from
larger to smaller craft to get close in shore to land. He had sampled the
landing craft himself, trying out the small galley, *Martin,* which held
only sixty seamen. On Monday, the 16th, he went ashore to the
soldiers. Then he wrote to Venables suggesting if Venables agreed to
capture the fort that was a mile-and-a-half to the west of the town, he
Penn would send a force against it and would appoint 'some ships to
amuse them at the same time, with ordnance which might peradventure
scare them from their guns'. But Venables did not agree; he decided to
march back to shore, despite Haines saying, 'If we go back we shall give
the enemy opportunities and if we go back and march here again we
shall be as tired as we are now.' But Venables replied he knew best and
would hear *nothing more* but retreat to Hine Harbour.

The sailing master's journal continues for the 18th day, a
Wednesday:

This morning general Venables came aboard of us to his Ladie and left
his army to themselves. 19th, Thursday. This day mortar pieces and
ammunishon [sic] landed readie to march but General Venables being
aboard of our ship and his wife to lie by his side, did not feel the
hardship of the soldiers that lie on ye sand entirely. 20th. This day
General Venables did indeed go ashore to his armie and our general
did tell Gen Venables if he would think well of it he would send two
or three ships to beat down the fort. Venables said NO, he did intend
to let this fort alone. But he did not go any farther than aboard our
ship to his lady.

Butler's official report to Cromwell gave a complete account of the
defeat of the army at Hispaniola and Venable's absolute refusal to
attempt further battle. 'The General Venables came on board the
Swiftsure and desired they might go to some of the English plantations;
but would not be persuaded to attempt anything upon Domingo more;
so that we moved the taking of Jamaica.'

The loveable Commissioner Winslow became a changed man after
the defeat at Santo Domingo. He knew that 'the English army had
suffered the most disgraceful defeat in West Indian history due far more
to its own misbehaviour and cowardice than any efforts of the enemy
and only sailors had done anything to redeem the shameful story'. W. B.
heard him say as much.

Four days later Winslow fell very ill. In the afternoon he was carried down to his cabin in the *Swiftsure* and that evening he died. His resistance to local fevers had been lowered by his feelings of shame. He told his man it had broken his heart. He was buried at sea the next day. The sailing-master adds, 'We made sail and bore away for Jamaica, *Our General being alomost choked for want of venting and telling the armee of their baseness; but he thought it wisdom rather to be silent and to give them all the encouragement he could lest they should do the like where we were going.*'

By 3rd May the army was all shipped. Captain Gregory Butler, Cromwell's Commissioner, sent to report back to the Protector full details of all proceedings, wrote an account of the passage to Jamaica 'The 3rd May, [we] set sail from Hispaniola, and the 10th came into the harbour of Jamaica, General Penn leading the way with his own ship; for after the miscarriage at Hispaniola, I have heard him say he would not trust the army with the attempt, if he could come near with his ships; and indeed did, in the *Martin* galley, run in till she was aground before the breastwork in the bottom of the harbour.'

General Venables watched this from the deck of the *Swiftsure* being 'much more cheerful than before'. The harbour, today known as Kingston Harbour is one of the largest natural harbours in the world. At that day reports said it would hold a thousand ships. The southern side of the harbour is formed by a narrow low lying arm of land. Ships went there to careen. Today on this strip aircraft land from all over the world. On the north-west corner of the harbour is a shallow bay, Hunt's Bay. It is where the river which comes past the capital, six miles further inland, enters the main harbour. Penn ran the *Martin* galley into this bay. Venables was at last persuaded to leave his wife and come aboard the *Martin,* which was piloted by a man who knew Hunt's Bay as well as the main harbour. Whistler reports

Our general commanded the boates to follow us with the men; our seamen running the boates fast aground and the soldiers leping in the water to wade ashore . . . but our army did not follow the ennimie but did resolve to stay until their general came ashore to them. For all this time he was raped up in his cloak with his hat over his eyes as if he was studying of fissick more than like a general of an army . . . But our generall did call encouragement, telling them that the ennemie did run. General V[enables]. seeing the enemy all fled and none there to oppose our armie did desire a boat saying he would go ashore to the armie where he found them all drawn up where they did resolve to camp this night and to take the day before them to march up to the town.

Despite Venables' delay, the town was easily captured. So Cromwell's soldiers, who had spent the night hearing frogs singing in the trees, the crabs sounding like bandilleros and flashing fireflies demoralising their sentries, while their bodies were eaten by mosquitos, were lucky for the first time since the expedition began. But their luck was not to last for long. Venables was no better a negotiator than he was as a soldier and by the time he realised he was being tricked by the Spaniards it was too late for him to do anything about it.

The Spaniards were astonished when Venables announced that he came not to pillage but to plant and to take possession of the island in the name of the Lord Protector of England, His Highness Oliver Cromwell. They were even more astonished at the extremely hard terms presented to them. First Venables demanded enough beef to feed his army and declared the governor himself must come; he would treat with no one else. But the governor was a long way away and a very sick old man who had to be carried in a hammock. So days passed while the Spaniards took the opportunity of hiding their treasures and driving their cattle into the hills. Venables, unaware of this, sent word to Penn that the town was captured and to come up as without him the treaty could not be signed.

'On Wednesday 16th, General Penn, having long considered the articles, left his approbation and returned to the fleet.' On 17th the Spaniards signed the articles. But no wonder Penn long considered the articles for they were incredibly harsh. All those who wished to leave the island might do so, taking only the clothes in which they stood; they would be transported with wives and families to some other Spanish port, but they must bring all their goods and money to an appointed place upon pain of death. However the Spaniards kept talking and meanwhile carried their goods away . . . 'The soldiers might starve [with] nothing to drink but water and so withing twelve days our men fell ill with bloody flux. By 30th May, 3,000 men were ill and dying every day.'

No responsible commander would have kept all his men in an island in those conditions. Some soldiers were needed to serve with their officers to maintain the English presence. Some ships and English sailors were needed, but the navy was not. Penn decided to sail for England.

London was then three months and nineteen sailing days away. A council of war was called. They decided the army had no need of help from so many ships. And finally, 'who knew but that enemies both without and within might lay hold of the opportunity of our absence, to rise and make attempts at home.'

This was very shrewd, because they had only just received the news that parliament had been dissolved. Cromwell, Lord Protector, would henceforth rule alone. No matter on which side seamen's personal sympathies might run, no one wanted to see England attacked and invaded by external enemies. Vice-Admiral Goodson was left behind to command the fleet remaining in Jamaica.

Setting sail on 25th June, the departing fleet gave itself an unlooked-for send-off. The *Discovery,* the third ship in Penn's squadron, was ordered to take aboard twenty-four guns and some carpenter's stores. The ensuing catastrophe is described in Penn's log, written aboard the *Fellowship* that very night.

This evening happened the sad accident of fire on board the *Discovery,* occasioned by drawing off brandy in the steward's room. The liquor took flame and gained so that at midnight she blew up, having in her 120 barrels of powder. but God, in His goodness carried the burning timbers to landward; and by the burning timbers, the wood was set on fire, and continued burning the next day.

The blazing mountainside of Jamaica must have made an amazing spectacle.

Penn's sailing master shrewdly assessed the situation they were leaving behind them: 'Now our Army did still remain in that sad condition of being half starved and visited with sickness; the Major General now had a longing to go to England. It is thought that he will not be long after us as his Ladie doth remain with him.' Whistler's prophecy proved true. Penn sailed on the 25th and Venables, afraid of what Penn might have written to the Protector and what he might say on arrival in London, sailed one month later.

On Thursday, 30th August, Penn's squadron saw land which was thought to be the Lizard and on the 31st, between four and five in the afternoon, they anchored at Spithead. Penn at once sent off 'an express', with a letter to the Lord Protector: 'May it please your Highness, As to my coming home, it was somewhat against my inclination to leave your Highness' service in these parts, but was advised that my departure for

England might be more requisite for your service than my stay there. I am now waiting only on your Highness' commands.'

Then followed three interminable days in the *Swiftsure* at anchor at Spithead. He had written similar letters to the commissioners of the Admiralty, and to General Disbrowe. He wrote to Disbrowe a second time, 'Honoured Sir, In my last to you I signified how I had informed his Highness that I then awaited his commands to come and yield him an account, but not having answer from His Highness, or yourself, I am in a strait what to do, but shall stay your answer. Sir, I shall desire, and not doubt, but your answer hereto will be very speedy, to your Most faithful W. P.'

Penn expected to be granted leave, as was customary after a long voyage and before or during that leave to visit the Protector and give his report. The letter which reached him is the very last in his ship's log. It was a curt command.

Sir, The council having notice of your arrival with the fleet; and also of the orders given by the commissioners of the Admiralty, and navy how ships be disposed of, do hold your presence here necessary, that they may receive information from you.

Signed in the name by order of the council

H. Lawrence, President

Whitehall, 3rd September, 1655

For General Wm Penn.

Accordingly, on 12th September, the very same day that an anxious Venables arrived at Portsmouth Bay, near Spithead, Penn attended the council and gave his report; every word of which Secretary John Thurloe wrote down. It is a repetition of the ship's log.

The examination was concluded with Penn's comments on the strategic value of Jamaica.

The island is for situation to annoy the Spaniard as low as the Honduras the best in America, it was much provided with provisions from thence. In Jamaica they kill eighty thousand hogs every year for their grease, vended at Cartagene. Ships can sail to and from Cartagene to this island in five days. There is an excellent river runs by the town, fresh water. The harbour is as good as ever he sailed in.

Penn was dismissed and the commissioners sat down to discuss 'the whole business of Jamaica and to report the state thereof, with their opinions, to the council.'

It was not till 20th September that judgement was given. Meanwhile Venables had been questioned on his arrival in London, some days after Penn. Cromwell himself attended this meeting, for it is stated that

His Highness acquainted the council that General Robert Venables attended the door, whereupon he was called in. ORDERED, That it be offered to his Highness, as the advice of the council that General Robert Venables be comitted to the Tower.

That it be offered to his highness, as the advice of the Council, that General William Penn be committed to the Tower.

The shock was great. Penn, summoned to the council, rose, drew his sword from its scabbard and leaving it on the table followed the guards to the water's edge and took boat from Westminster to the Tower. Once there he entered by the Main Gate, known as the Traitor's Gate, though it was used for many purposes, the river being the highway of London. Samuel Pepys' story of the admiral sitting crying in a dungeon in the Tower, like any common seaman, is utterly false. As the present Resident Governor and Keeper of the Jewel House, H. M. Tower of London, Major-General D. M. Raeburn, points out, 'Penn was lodged in the Lieutenants' Lodgings . . . he was after all, a State prisoner, and only State prisoners were put in the Tower. He would be treated with respect and have some modest comfort. Also in those days the Tower had no dungeons. Ordinary prisoners of lesser rank were put into prisons which had dungeons not into the Tower.' What is true is that the fever he had contracted in Jamaica made him shiver with ague and misery without sight of his family. But within one week Margaret Penn, William and little Peg were in a lodging house on Tower Hill.

Cromwell was shattered by the failure of his great western design. Jamaica meant nothing to him. It had no gold to fill his coffers. His disappointment was so severe that his royalist enemies declared with delight that Cromwell had fallen down in a fit of convulsion at the news. True or not, Cromwell soon learned that the capture of Jamaica was being publicly acclaimed by the general public who read of *A great and wonderful victory obtained by the English Forces under the command of General Penn and General Venables* printed above an impressive woodcut of sailing ships at sea by Humphrey Hutchinson, in London, April, 1655. While Cromwell was digesting this fact, Penn remained sick and heartbroken at his unexpected treatment. It was on Tower Hill below these lieutenants' quarters that he formerly walked, gave orders, dispensed favours. He had captured a fertile and strategically valuable island. Cromwell was too intelligent not to begin to realise the commercial value of the island as he recalled the long questioning of Penn about it by the Commissioners. So he issued a *Proclamation of the Protector relating to Jamaica,*

> Whereas by the good providence of God, our fleet, in the late Expedition into America, have propted themselves of an island called Jamaica, Spacioys in extent, commodious in harbours, fertile . . . fit and worth to be planted and improved to the advantage and interest of the nation. And whereas divers persons, merchants and others are desirous to undertake and proceed upon plantations, on that island . . . we have ordered that every adventurer to that island shall be exempt from paying any excise or custim for any manufacture, or necessaries which they shall transport to Jamaica within the space of seven years from Michaelmas next.'

Cromwell knew that he might lose Blake's loyalty were he to cause revolt in the Navy by ill-treating the Admiral they loved and respected. If he kept Penn in the Tower he would certainly lose their respect and obedience, and with it, his own position. So an order was issued that if Penn and Venables were to write a letter of submission, they would be set free.

Penn, however, assured Cromwell 'that he would not in the manner expected, own himself in fault; yet for reasons best known to himself and the persuasion of others near the protector's person, he made his submission.

On 25th October Penn wrote a letter which, far from admitting failure or error, was dignified in the extreme.

> Being honoured with the command of the fleet in the late American Expedition, I returned home without leave, for which I have incurred your displeasure, and this is more displeasing to me than any wordly cross. My heart bears me witness that my return was not through refractoriness against superiors, but for advancement of the service. As I was first willing to part with all that was dear to me to help forward this Christian design, I would rather never have gone, if I thought my return made it less hopeful. I beg release from restraint on account of my family and my increasing distemper. It is the infirmity of man to err, but the virtue of a prince to pardon error.

Had Cromwell not already regretted his action against Penn, this letter would not have won his forgiveness. As it was he ordered his release on the same day. But there was a backlash. Penn had to resign his commission and give it to the hands of Mr. Jessop, a clerk of the Council. Mr. Jessop's account to his Highness and council reports coldly that 'he had received General Penn's commission and had thereupon delivered to the Lieutenant of the Tower, his Highness' warrant for General Penn's discharge.'

Penn was home at Chigwell a few hours after his release. The overwhelming joy with which he was received went far to mitigate the sufferings and disgrace they had shared in common, Margaret his dear wife, who had feared for his life in the Tower, and William, aged eleven. Little Peg was only three, but even she might have sensed the unhappiness of a home deprived of a father, and a hero cheated of his just renown. As to young William he dedicated his life to the God who had given them back their beloved father; his father's return was really the birth of the future Quaker.

The Admiral's salary as general of the fleet ended with the day he resigned his commission, and he had not received one penny for his conquest of Jamaica although his officers received grants of land in that island. Penn was reduced to nothing save the rents from his estates in Ireland. Cromwell had not deprived him of these, so he took his family to Ireland, where his royalist friends in Munster secretly cherished a hope of the king's return. Whether or not Penn had seriously contemplated diverting his fleet to the royalist camp, his late unwarranted disgrace and removal to Ireland confirmed his drift into royalist circles. There, farming his estates, which he had never yet seen, Jamaica became a memory in the joy of reunion with his family.

He could not know what the Dutch ambassador to London had written home: 'I endeavoured to speak to Mr Thurloe and told him, if the English had suffered in India, the *Dutch* had suffered more in Barbados under Admiral Penn.' Indeed, Penn had done more than merely accelerate the dissolution of the Spanish main. He had pre-empted for England, at the cost of our other maritime rivals, the major stake in the fragments.

CHAPTER SIX

Peace and the Restoration

The idea of removing to Ireland was additionally attractive to Penn because of Penn's great friendship with Broghill, who was now president of Munster. So it was arranged that Penn and his family should travel with Broghill and his family to Kinsale on the same boat. Penn also took with him a tutor for his son William, now almost twelve years of age. In addition he had two momentoes of Jamaica, Jack, the negro, afterwards known to Pepys as the admiral's 'Black', and a brilliant green parrot which General Venables had presented to him before he sailed from Jamaica.

It was all such familiar waters and hinterland to both men, if not to Margaret Penn, whose home had been further north, but it was no longer a place of great danger. Cromwell had subdued, imprisoned, sent overseas and confiscated the property of the rebellious Irish Catholics. Now there were many contented English settlers in this beautiful country.

Cromwell had given Penn the Castle of Macroom near Cork which had been the home of the Earl of Clancarty, formerly Lord Muskerry, whom Penn had fought in Ireland. It stands on the banks of the river Sullane and the setting sun fills its great rooms with a diffused light which may have influenced young William with a sense of divine glory when he listened to Thomas Loe, the Quaker, preach to the family and servants; for he wrote later, that the thought, 'What if we were all to become Quakers?' had just come into his head, when he saw tears pouring down Black Jack's face.

According to the records of the Irish Quakers, it was most probably owing to the influence of Penn's beloved wife, Margaret, who had previously shown some interest in Quakers, that, when a small group of them were travelling through the area, preaching, the Admiral 'decided to be like the noble Berean and hear him before he judged'. So it came about that the Oxford tradesman Thomas Loe and the group with him were invited into the great castle. Ten years later the same Thomas Loe brought about William's conversion to the Quakers. At their first meeting, the boy was absorbed by study. But he had felt his first glimpse of the indwelling spirit.

The admiral wasted no time at Macroom. He devoted himself to farming efficiently and did so well that he was soon able to buy neighbouring estates around him. He had already bought lands in Muskerry and County Cork from Broghill and the result of these transactions together with his careful work and planning put up the value of his estates from £300 to £838 per annum. A fortune today.

Yet, wherever he was, Penn never lost touch with Bristol. The merchant business set up by his father and uncle seems to have been continued and carried on by his cousins. It is certain that the Admiral and his wife had friends there for it is on record that Margaret Penn applied to a Quaker captain, Daniel Baker, for a passage when she wished to cross to Bristol for a visit in April, 1657.

Meanwhile Cromwell declared war on Spain officially. Blake, now aged sixty, was sent to the Mediterranean with Cromwell's admirer, Colonel Montagu (later to become the Earl of Sandwich), to learn seamanship. At Santa Cruz, off Tenerife, Blake won his last victory against the Spaniards. But returning home, he died on board his flagship the *George,* just as he was entering Plymouth Sound, on 7th August, 1657. He was given a state burial in Westminster Abbey on September 4th after having laid in State at Greenwich. The news reached Penn at Macroom.

Cromwell, realising that he was now without a good sea-general, must have recalled Penn to the navy some time during the following eleven months, for the Dutch ambassador to England wrote to the States General on 9th March, 1658,

High and Mighty Lords, My Lords, since my last, here are letters come from the fleet under General Pen, advising, that the same was in very great danger, through a violent tempest, wherewith they were almost driven upon the shore, it being very misty weather, so they could not see whereabouts they were; and if so be that one of the foremost of the fleet, a small vessel, had not perceived a high cliff by a sudden flash of light, which presently turned and gave notice to all the next, they had all been stranded and lost.

Whether or not the ambassador knew it, they were in fact preparing for their assault on the important enemy port of Dunkirk.

The capitulation of the Spanish garrison at Dunkirk to the combined forces of the English and French three months later, in June, and delivered up by Louis XIV and Mazarin in person was to make a fitting last triumph for the Lord Protector Cromwell. The two French dignitaries came on board the *Naseby,* which was commanded by Montagu. Little did any of those present imagine that the very same ship, renamed the *Royal Charles* was to bring back the king to the throne of England so soon. For Cromwell did not long outlive this satisfactory victory. He died on 3rd September, a very great Englishman, idolised and cursed from that day to this, according to the temperament and political disposition of the person considering him. His secretary, Thurloe, in announcing his death to his son, Henry Cromwell, wrote, 'I am not able to speak or write; this stroke is so sore, so unexpected, so stupendous . . . never was there any man so prayed for during his sickness.' While the diarist John Evelyn wrote, 'The 22nd October I saw the superb funeral of the Protector; it was the joyfullest funeral that ever I saw, for there were none that cried but dogs, which the soldiers hooted away, drinking and taking tobacco in the streets as they went.' Whichever point of view is adopted, it can never be forgotten that it was the navy and its victories, not Cromwell's battles on land, which made him famous in the eyes of foreigners and England once more a force to be contended with.

The dying Cromwell had nominated his eldest son Richard as his successor, but as his friend and official adviser Broghill said, 'Richard had neither genius nor friends, nor treasure, nor army to support him.' In less than one month, 'poor Tumble-Down Dick' and his parliament were ignored. This behaviour kept all the country in a state of ceaseless turbulence and – in a graphic phrase of Granville Penn's – 'a general longing prevailed that the key-stone should at length be restored to the shattered arch of the kingdom.'

Penn decided that his place was no longer on the flag-ship in the Mediterranean, where Cromwell had sent him, but at home. The time had come for him to play his part in restoring law and order. Since the death of Blake, he was, as he well knew, the most powerful sailor-commander in the navy and that it was to him and no one else, that the seamen looked for their final orders. Some years previously when the navy declared its loyalty to the country it served, the wording used was 'to the government of king and parliament'. The government of king and parliament must now be re-established if civil war was to be avoided. As he sailed out of the Mediterranean Penn could at last speak his mind openly to his fellow officers and the seamen round him and word spread easily from ship to ship. 'There must be no more military dictators in England. . . the king must be restored, by a freely elected parliament.'

Penn decided to sail to Bristol for his plans were forming fast. His first thoughts were to approach his native city and suggest becoming its member of parliament. In May the Junta had recalled the Rump, but as intelligent men knew, the Rump would never recall the king.

A necessary qualification for a prospective M.P. was to be a free burgess. In the council minutes of Bristol there is a reference to a committee being appointed to consider Penn's application. The records show that Giles Penn (his father) was a free burgess so Penn was admitted in the usual way. But he was not then elected to become an M.P. for Bristol, because in May 1659 Bristol elected as its representatives two Aldermen, Robert Aldsworth and Miles Jackson. Penn was the unsuccessful candidate amongst three contestants.

The result is less surprising than it seems when one remembers that Bristol was more a trading city than a naval port. In fact, his defeat was fortunate, for the padded Rump was wholly unsatisfactory during the troubled winter of 1659/60, so that he was better out of it. Weymouth was a naval town and welcomed the victor of the Battle of Portland when he applied to be made a Burgess of Weymouth and gladly chose him to be their candidate. Meanwhile Bristol was a good centre for propaganda. Penn was in constant touch with ships at sea, with Lawson in the Downs and with Broghill in Ireland, as well as with the strong loyalist Ormonde who was with the heir to the throne overseas. Things were going well for the king in many quarters. The day when Penn would be able to pronounce openly in favour of a Restoration appeared to be drawing near.

The navy's role in the Restoration has frequently been under-estimated or ignored. Naval intervention was decisive at two points. First, in December, 1659, Vice-Admiral Lawson and his captains acted to prevent an extension of military rule by sailing for London in support of the recall of parliament. Although the fleet's attitude at that stage evinced no overt royalism, it made the Restoration possible by undermining military dictatorship, the only viable long-term alternative to monarchy. At the time, no other force to uphold the constitutional against the dictatorial cause was present in the decisive arena: General George Monck was still in Scotland; the city fathers of London, though courageous in their opposition to the army, had no effective militia of their own. Thus until Monck arrived to hold the ring in February, 1660, it was Lawson's guns which presided over the dissolution of army rule.

Secondly, between February and April, 1660, when Monck was in effective control of England's destiny, knowledge of the navy's stance helped him make up his own naturally vacillating mind, resolving first on the re-admission of moderate members, previously excluded, to the House of Commons, and then on new parliamentary elections, which, in the prevailing mood across the country, would be sure to return a royalist majority.

Penn's role, spinning a web of communications from his Bristol bastion or his Irish fastness, can only be glimpsed. But it was evidently of the highest importance. Sir Harry Vane, unwavering in his republicanism and therefore in his support for the army chiefs, rated his old friend's influence highly enough to try to persuade him to use it in favour of the good old cause. Penn must have been involved in the formulation of an invitation the king received from Broghill early in 1660 to make his entry into his recovered realm through Ireland. The new parliament, when it met, recognised Penn's part in the king's cause by choosing him to sail in the *Naseby* to Scheveningen to welcome Charles II in the name of parliament and accompany him back to his kingdom.

Penn, of course, was a member of that parliament. On 6th April, the corporation of Weymouth wrote to inform him of his election: 'Sir, The Freeholders of this town have chosen your honour and the Lord-General Montagu burgesses for the Borough of Weymouth, for the ensuing Parliament. It was very much to our satisfaction that the election passed with so much cheerfulness and unanimity . . . When parliament assembled, Penn was the only sailor in it.

The new Parliament met on 25th April 1660, 'in the nineteenth year of the reign of Charles II' and succeeding years are numbered accordingly. Parliament was summonded to meet 'at Westminster at ten o'clock in the forenoon and repaired to St Margaret's, Westminster, to hear a sermon preached by Dr Reignolds, and that being ended they repaired to the Parliament House, went in and sat in their places.' Their first work was to choose a Speaker. Sir Harbottle Grimston was unanimously acclaimed. He was conducted to the Chair by Lord General Monck. When he sat down, the Mace was called for, brought in by the Sergeant and placed on the table. The historic piece of play-acting smothered with panoply the doubtful legitimacy of this parliament's origins.

On 1st May Sir John Granville came to the door of the House of Commons with a letter from Charles. The whole House rose to its feet as the letter was read out by the Speaker. It began 'Trusty and well-beloved . . . we greet you all . . . We do assure you upon our royal word that this is our opinion of Parliaments that their authority is most necessary for the government of the kingdom'. This tone of reconciliation was sustained, and the Restoration assured. On the vexed question of religion Charles' letter continued, 'If you desire the advancement and propagating of the Protestant Religion . . . we have by our constant profession and practice of it, given sufficient testimony to the world.'

On 8th May parliament invited the king to return. 'Resolved et nemine contradicte.'

The *Naseby* was the ship chosen to fetch back the king. Parliament gave orders for a standard of silk, also a jack, an ensign, a suit of pendants, a waft cloth, all to be made of silk, to decorate it. For the king's own person parliament ordered a rich bed of velvet, embroidered in gold, with a High Chair of State and rich coach. It became the duty of Penn and Montagu to see that all orders concerning the fleet were carried out.

Lord General Montagu, the second M.P. for Weymouth, was a valiant soldier who had been made General-at-Sea by Cromwell, though he knew nothing whatever about the sea. He had changed sides without conspicuously enlarging his talents, after Cromwell's death. He went on board the *Naseby* on 30th March, when he had been comissioned to command the fleet, and on 4th April Penn joined his fellow M.P. for dinner in the General's cabin. It is the first mention of Penn made by Samuel Pepys, then Montagu's secretary.

On 11th May, Montagu reported that he was already in the Downs and wrote, 'That I might be in a better capacity to receive His majesty's commands, I am now under sail for the bay of Scheveningen in

Holland.' The ships *Naseby, London, Swiftsure, Richard, Plymouth, Essex, Winsby, Foresight, Yarmouth* and *Lark* composed the fleet which, next day, stood out to sea together. Penn, however, was not on board. He had separate orders: on 16th May, while considering the public revenue, Parliament awarded him 'one hundred pounds for a special service, to be charged on the treasury of the navy'. The special service was 'to hasten to the fleet with such ships as are here in the river or at Portsmouth' and proceed to the rendez-vous off Scheveningen where he would board the *Naseby* and join General Montagu. When the monarch stepped on deck, Penn was to bid the king of England welcome on behalf of parliament. It was the greatest honour which parliament could give at that time to any of its members.

Penn was piped aboard the *Naseby* before they reached Scheveningen, but the sea was so rough it was four days before the Duke of York, the new Lord High Admiral, could come on board to take possession of his fleet. He was young and better-looking than the king and had more experience as a soldier, but he knew nothing about the sea. Unlike his brother King Charles, he took his new duties very seriously, and was determined to learn all he could about seamanship in order to fill the post of Lord High Admiral in as worthy a manner as possible.

The Duke brought his secretary on board with him, William Coventry. Coventry and Penn had a mutual friend in Lord Ormonde; it was through Ormonde that Coventry applied to Penn for advice, quickly discovering that he and Penn had the same standards of honour in a venal age. Clarendon, who soon grew jealous of them both, wrote that with admiral Penn 'Mr Coventry made a fast friendship and was guided in all things.' Through Coventry, Penn was naturally brought into close touch with the Duke of York with the result that, just as sixteen years before, on shipboard, a lifelong friendship began between Penn and his passenger, Lord Broghill, so on this cross-channel run an equally lasting friendship sprang up between the young duke and Penn. Based at first on Penn's wit and friendliness, some hero-worship crept in, for was not this General the only life-long sailor of rank? The one so greatly admired on the continent for his defeat of the Dutch? As both Penn and the duke were passengers on the *Naseby* they had plenty of time to discuss naval questions in detail as they strolled on the decks together. This new friendship was to have incalculable results for the fortunes of Penn and his family, for the duke's loyalty was to prove outstanding and surprise the world. It soon became a cause of jealousy among those who were not Penn's friends.

On 23rd May the king came on board the *Naseby,* and as he climbed the gangway, Penn in his full dress uniform, with rosette, lace ruffles, silk sash and sword, stood at the entering port to receive him. Sweeping off his tricorne with a wide gesture as he made his obeisance, Penn bade the king welcome on behalf of the parliament of England. At which, King Charles drew his sword from its scabbard and knighted Admiral Penn, where he knelt on the deck. Yet Pepys in his *Diary* makes no mention of the event at all. It is the historian Lord Clarendon who records that 'as soon as he came on board the king knighted Admiral Penn.' Was jealousy already stirring in the breast of Montagu's secretary? Perhaps, alternatively, Clarendon's story is another *canard* and Penn's only knighting was that conferred by Henry Cromwell in 1658.

Pepys recounts dispassionately enough the alteration of some embarrassing ships' names. 'After dinner the king and duke altered the name of some of the ships, including the *Naseby* into *Charles;* the *Richard, James;* the *Speaker, Mary* . . . That done we weighed anchor and with a fresh gale set sail for England. Dryden echoed him in a more lapidary formula:

> The *Naseby* now no longer England's shame
> But better to be lost in Charles's name
> Received her lord.

The *Charles* reached Dover on the morning of the 25th May. Pepys wrote, 'I spoke with the duke about business . . . Great expectations of the king making some knights, but there was none.' This second chance of mentioning that one had already been made is not taken. He goes on to describe the king being received on shore by General Monck. Afterwards, the king entered a stately coach and drove to Canterbury and London. But Penn and Sir William Batten and Pepys made their way back to the ship.

In the House of Commons the king was loyally received in speech after speech. The most gracious of all was that of the Speaker in his thanks to Montagu, 'My Lord, you have landed our sovereign upon the safest shores that ever English king set his foot upon . . . the hearts of his people.' Montagu's reward was to be made the Earl of Sandwich.

Pepys overcame his sea-sickness but he never overcame his growing jealousy of Penn, troubled, as he admitted, 'out of envy' to see Penn consulted by the heir to the throne. Fear that Penn would always eclipse his patron and protector was always in his mind, for Penn was an infinitely more distinguished naval commander than Sandwich. To understand how this strange double rivalry came about in Samuel Pepys's mind it is essential to understand something of Pepys's origins. He was the son of a tailor; his mother was the sister of a butcher; but Samuel's father's aunt had married Sir Sidney Montagu whose family were amongst the richest in the country. Montagu was attracted to young Samuel by his outstanding intelligence and put him through St Paul's school and Magdalene College, Cambridge. Then he made him his secretary and finally took him to sea. Sandwich then used his powers to have Pepys created Clerk of the Acts to the newly appointed commissioners of the Navy Board. In addition he advised Pepys that it was not the salary of the place that did make a man rich, but the opportunity of getting money while he is in the place.' Pepys acted on the advice and made a great fortune which he regularly recorded in his *Diary* so that it was also his account book. Money was his standard of judgement; honesty was Penn's. This incompatibility did nothing to turn Pepys's pretended friendship towards Penn into a genuine one: 'Though I do not love him.' Pepys wrote, 'yet I find it necessary to keep in with him.' Hepworth Dixon, writing in 1856, said, 'It was the admiral's misfortune to be portrayed chiefly through the outpourings and petty jealousies of his famous detractor and pretended friend, Samuel Pepys, who was proud to be seen with him . . . eager to take Lady Penn and her daughter for a river trip . . . and then retire to his garret to describe his official superior with vituperation.' In his brilliant biography of Pepys, Richard Ollard pinpoints this jealousy as totally irrational. Pepys averred that he did 'hate him and his traitorous tricks with all my heart'. Penn was 'a rogue at heart . . . a counterfeit rogue, . . . a false knave', corrupt, envious, lazy, dissembling, boorish, hypocritical in religion, atheistical, boorish, unchaste and 'of very mean parts but only a bred seaman'. Pepys, in short, entertains amply, but protests too much.

Two days after he set foot in London, the king held his first Council in Whitehall, May 31st, 1660. Those present included the Duke of York, Lord General Monck, Admiral Penn and some thirteen others. His Majesty ordered the commissioners to issue monies for the necessities of the navy until further orders.

Penn knew how desperately the navy needed money and what a great load of debt the king had inherited from Cromwell's navy. He was also greatly concerned with the way navy money had been handled during the years of his service and knew that four commissioners could not be left to supervise the finance of their section. It was not possible and opened the doors to corruption. He was also aware that despite their interest in the navy, neither the Lord High Admiral nor the king knew anything about naval affairs. Penn therefore wrote a paper, entitled *Form of Government of the Navy* and personally presented it to the king in June 1660. The king and duke read it and then appointed a committee to consider it.

In brief, the paper made a series of suggestions about 'how the navy should be governed to His Majesty's best advantage and profit.' In the past the navy had four principal officers, Treasurer, Comptroller, Surveyor and Clerk of the Records, with clerks beneath them. These were sufficient when the navy was small; but now the navy was large . . . nearly 160 sail – and the expense vast, 'It is thought by those who know that the best and safest way for his Majesty's service is to govern the navy by commissioners. 1. THE TREASURER. 2. THE COMP-TROLLER. 3 THE SURVEYOR. 4. CLERK OF THE RECORDS OR ACTS. But he ought to be an excellent accountant, well versed in naval affairs otherwise gross errors may ensue.' In this advice we hear Penn, the merchant adventurer, speaking; he knew how to ensure shipping profits were not embezzled. Now he applied this to the navy by insisting that accounts and contracts were closely scrutinised 'by enacting that principal officers be reduced to commissioners to sit in a joint body'. Pepys certainly – and, more surprising, Sir George Cartaret, treasurer to the navy – became very angry indeed when found they were to have their accounts looked into.

Penn's paper convinced the king and duke: 'it was ordered by his Majesty in council, that his said Royal Highness, the Lord High Admiral, do appoint and authorise John, Lord Berkeley, Sir William Penn, knight, Peter Pett, Esquire, to be commissioners for the navy.' They were to join with Sir George Cartaret, treasurer, Sir William Batten, surveyor, now brought out of retirement, and the much-loved, garrulous old Sir John Minnes, comptroller of the board. Samuel Pepys was to assist the newly appointed commissioners, as Clerk of the Acts – in modern terms, to act as secretary to the board, recording the minutes of meetings. It was also provided that the shipbuilder, Peter Pett, 'be not obliged to a continual attendance jointly with all other officers, but that his chief care be employed at Chatham, the place of his ordinary residence'. Salaries were also fixed. The treasurer, Sir George Cartaret, was paid £2,000 per annum. He had reconquered his native island of Jersey for the king during the civil war and sheltered Charles II there as well as Clarendon. An able sea-officer, he was now rewarded. Penn was given £500 a year. Pett and Pepys each had £350 a year; to be paid quarterly. In addition each of these officers was given a house in Navy Gardens and Pepys was put in charge of the gardens. Here the commissioners and their families would walk and converse together, discuss gossip from the court, news of shipping, or Holland. On fine nights Penn would come out on the leads of his house and listen to his next door neighbour Pepys playing his flageolet in the moonlight.

By adding Penn to the Navy Board, the king had greatly strengthened it. Of the original generals-at-sea, only three remained, Monck, Penn and Montagu. But Monck and Montagu were land-generals, of whom the seaman's joke about the landsmen's commands, 'Wheel right . . . wheel left' was even more amusing than it sounds today, as ships had no steering wheel before 1700, only the whiplash on which the helmsman pulled. Batten and Cartaret were seamen of experience, but neither had commanded a squadron of the fleet in battle. Of all the commissioners, Penn was the only one who had. Clarendon was angry and jealous, on two accounts. He thought the creation of the Navy Board belittled the power of his son-in-law, the Lord High Admiral. Secondly, he was jealous of the duke's friendship with Penn, though he was honest enough to write, when the next Dutch war began, 'His Highness consulted daily with Sir John Lawson, Sir George Ayscue and Sir William Penn, all men of great experience and who had commanded in battles.'

The work of the Navy Board, meanwhile, was purely practical. Its function was to produce ships . . . hence the wisdom of having that great ship-builder, Pett, on the board. Also it had to find everything needed to sail those ships and repair them. Sails, masts, anchors, flags, spars and small boats for the large ships and guns for battle. Ships needed provisions of every kind from water, beer and food down to candles and gunpowder. The Navy Board also had to recruit trained experts, the ships' sailing masters, boatswains, carpenters, cooks, as well as the gunners and purser.

The officers were appointed by the Lord High Admiral and in this, the Duke of York and later the king, took great personal interest. So did Penn; and the Lord High Admiral leaned heavily on Penn's judgement during the second Dutch war. From lifelong and bitter experience Penn knew every aspect of a ship's needs, and – more than that – of the crew's needs. The necessity of a good surgeon was something he always stressed and fought to have. He knew what sufferings shortages could cause. Above all he was conscious of the financial temptations offered to men of little conscience, when it came to ships' supplies. He knew the necessity of close examination of quality as well as quantity and knew how seamen could suffer from the profits made unjustifiably by secret agreements made between merchants and those in power to offer contracts. His insistence on personally examining the work of the dockyards and suppliers was later to infuriate Pepys, for it greatly affected that gentleman's pocket.

But men were more important than ships in the final outcome of any action at sea. Penn knew what it meant when wages could not be paid: first their sufferings, and that of their families, followed by desertion, and, to replace them, the terrible recourse of the press gang. Worst of all was when merchant ships returning to an English port were boarded and men forcibly taken off them for the navy, before they could be given their share of prize money after the sale of prizes on shore.

Chances of peculation came Penn's way and must have tempted him, for he was committed, like Pepys, to trying to build up an impressive patrimony. In a letter to his son dated 17th July, 1666, Penn mentioned the office of Governor and Captain of the Castle and Fort of Kinsale in Ireland and captaincy of a foot company there which the king had given him in 1660. 'Beside the ancient title it gives of Admiral of Ireland,' he remarks 'it is worth to any man that would attend to it, 400£ per annum.' But Penn had little time to be in Ireland, so it was honour without cash. If Pepys heard of it he ignored it, though he misses few chances to accuse Penn of sharing his own greed. His next reference captures the tone of playful banter which alternates with vitriol in his accounts of his relations with Penn. 1st November, 1660: 'This morning Sir William Penn and I were mounted early . . . We came to Sir William Batten's (at Walthamstow) where he lives like a prince . . . Among other things he showed us . . . a chaire which he calls King Harry's chaire, where he that sits down is catched with two irons that come round about him, which makes good sport.'

Until October 1660 Penn seems to have lived the life of a lonely bachelor in London. His great friend, Sir Harry Vane, had been banished to his estates in Northumberland and the uncertain situation in London after the Restoration made it safer for Penn's family to remain at Macroom Castle. Despite the many celebrations of joy in the capital there was much bitterness in the land. The king had granted a general pardon, but in the years of political and religious persecution, Roman Catholics, Quakers, and members of the Church of England, had all in turn been deprived of their lands. Even the estates of the king and of bishops were taken back from their new owners in England, Scotland and Ireland.

Scotland hated English control in the guise of a union of parliaments and returned to the old relation of two separate estates united only by the crown. In Ireland the question was even more difficult, how to satisfy alike the recent English immigrants who had received lands from Cromwell and the Irish proprietors whose land had been taken from them for supporting the king, and given to the English. A map of Ireland called *The Donne Survey* of forfeited estates cost £1,000, engraved in Amsterdam, according to Evelyn. There was therefore no doubt as to which lands had been given to the English. The king took a great interest in this and in 1661 an Act of Settlement was passed, making, in elaborate detail, a genuine attempt to satisfy all the claimants. The Irish had a House of Parliament, but the majority of members were Protestants of English descent. The result was that whereas before 1641 about two thirds of arable land had been in Catholic hands, in the reign of Charles II two thirds were held by Protestants. This did not, however, save Penn from having to hand back his Irish estates, the Castle of Macroom and the lands which he had bought and cultivated; for Macroom Castle belonged to Charles's friend, the Earl of Clancarty, a Roman Catholic, who had commanded the rebellious Irish troops. In return Penn was given an estate at Shanaggarry in the Barony of Imokilly in East Cork, and Konakilty, West Cork and also made governor and captain of the castle and fort at Kinsale. This involved detailed legal business which had to be attended to by Lady Penn in his absence.

Because Penn had taken over Macroom he came under the class of men to be 'pardoned'. All men had been pardoned by the king on his accession. But the admiral had served under Cromwell and this in the eyes of countless royalists was a grave thing to have done. Feelings ran high, as is evidenced by the fury of vengeance not only on Cromwell, but Ireton and Bradshaw, who were dug up and hanged, and the bodies of Blake and Pym, which were taken out of the abbey and flung into a pit outside.

Therefore it was wiser for Penn to have his own personal pardon. With great delicacy the king saw to it, and it was presented to Penn, fifteen days before the coronation on 23rd April, 1661. In its form it was more like a decoration than a pardon. Inscribed in Latin it is a thing of exquisite beauty, worthy of being hung in a gallery of art treasures. It is engraved on sheepskin about three foot by two and a half. The top left hand corner has the king's head framed in an eight-inch oval of flowers. The royal arms, horses, majestic lions, frail insects, roses, thistles, periwinkles, butterflies, snails and honey bees form a wide border that delights the eye. The wording was general. It included all treasons, 'transgressions relating to war authorised by . . . our father (Charles I) or other person called Lord Protector'. A later section refers to exceptions, mentioning rebellion in Ireland.

Three months after Penn's pardon, his friend, Sir Harry Vane, as an unrepentant republican, was put in prison and then, to Penn's great grief, was executed. Vane had withdrawn from parliament in 1648; republican though he was, he objected to putting the king on trial and absented himself. But unfortunately he returned to office on the day of the king's execution. This fact was used against him. Pepys thought Vane died nobly. Huge stands were erected for the public to attend the spectacle of the executions near the Tower and in Whitehall, as if for a football match. No wonder Penn was glad his family were living in Ireland.

As Penn could not go to Ireland, he began to discuss his elder son's future with Ormonde. William would be sixteen on 14th October that year and his father wanted him to have a better education than he had at that age. Ormonde suggested Christ Church, Oxford. William was accepted as a gentleman commoner, not only for his name, but also for his work. He had done particularly well in Latin. He was tall, athletic and, like his father, 'he was fecetious in conversation'.

Penn sent for his son to come to London and took him to court where he was well received both for his father's sake and his own good manners and lack of obsequiousness. Penn must have enjoyed the few days leave which he took to accompany his son to Oxford, riding through the leafy lanes of Buckinghamshire, where Penn relations still owned the estates of their ancestors. Penn rejoiced that his son was going to be something more than a 'tarpaulin'.

On his arrival at Oxford, William had a great stroke of luck. The students were invited to commemorate in Latin the death of the king's youngest brother, the Duke of Gloucester, from smallpox six weeks before, in the midst of the festivities. The king was heartbroken and the sadness of the event touched William and his father. William set to work and wrote his Latin elegy, the first verse of which was

> Publica te, Dux magne, dabant jejunia genti.
> Sed facta est, nato principe, festa dies.
> Te Moriente, licet celebraret laeta triomphos
> Anglia, solemnes solvitur in lachrymas.
> Solus ad arbitrium moderaris pectora. Solus
> Tu dolor accedis, deliciaeque tuis.

Thomas Clarkson, his first biographer, translated it in 1813;

> Though 'twas a Fastday when thou cam'st, thy birth
> Turned it at once to festive mirth.
> Though England at thy death, still made her show
> Of public joy, she passed to public woe.
> Thou dost alone the public breast control
> Alone bring joy or sorrow to the soul.

The king and the Duke of York were delighted with it and openly said so in court, but Pepys does not mention it.

From 1651 to 1660 Christ Church had as Dean Dr John Owen, a broad-minded non-conformist, whom Cromwell had appointed. After the Restoration he was replaced by Dr Reynolds who brought back high church ritual, and ordered the wearing of surplices. But Dr Owen lived near Oxford and held religious meetings in his house, where he encouraged students to resist and abhor 'popish innovations'. Dr Owen was a friend of Lord Broghill, who introduced William Penn to him.

Under the Puritans all Christmas festivities had been forbidden and parliament sat on Christmas Day 1660. It was dissolved 29th December and called for 8th May. It became known as the Cavalier Parliament. Admiral Penn was again chosen for the Borough of Weymouth and

Melcombe Regis, for which he sat until his death. The coronation of Charles II offered a splendid chance to send to Oxford for his son to come and join him for the celebrations. Penn hired the house of Mr Young, the flag-maker, for the great procession on the day preceding the coronation. Triumphal arches were erected on the route, the naval arch being in Cornhill near the Exchange. The flag-maker's house was in Cornhill and gave a perfect view. Here Sir William and Lady Batten joined Penn and his handsome son William with their own two daughters, as well as Samuel Pepys and his wife.

The next morning was that of the coronation, so Pepys makes no mention of the Penns. The admiral was not with the party in Cornhill. Penn, as one of the three admirals and generals at sea, had an official place in the Abbey, and probably his wife and son also. Pepys went to the abbey at four in the morning and, climbing up into the huge scaffolding at the north end, sat there until eleven o'clock when the king came in. The ancient ceremony of the coronation as Pepys describes it is the same pageant seen in our day, with the bishops, the King of Arms and his proclamation, the royal heralds, etc. Then a general pardon was read by the Lord Chancellor. At last Pepys went home. 'When it fell a thundering and lightning later, he and his wife hoped to see the fireworks, but they were not performed, because of the rain. Only the city had a light like a glory round about it with bonfires.'

During his coronation leave from Oxford, William was again taken to court and introduced as the author of the poetic elegy to the first Duke of Gloucester. He was now a tall, strong youth, smartly dressed in courtier fashion and he wore a sword. He made a good impression from the first and Penn foresaw a good future for his son won with far less hardship than his own had been.

A new and happy era had started. The day parliament opened Penn had the pleasure of attending with Batten, recently elected for Rochester when he and Lady Batten had ridden out to meet him with the good news. Sir George Cartaret and Sir William Coventry were also M.P.s At last there were four members to speak up for the needs of the navy and the Navy Board.

But William was not so happy to return to Oxford. When orders came from the crown that all undergraduates must wear surplices, many took them off after service and went drinking and gambling. If they kept them on there was always a crowd of students waiting to tear them off by force. It is believed William joined gaily in. But later after attending lectures on body and soul, he became thoughtful and started to ride out to Dr Owen's house for prayer and sacred singing. Soon he stopped going to chapel, preferring Dr Owen to Dr Fell. The heads of all the colleges sent for Owen's students and fined the delinquents for nonconformity.

When the news reached the admiral's ears, Penn ordered his son to come to Navy Gardens immediately. In the matter of discipline he was very much a shipboard captain. William was severely admonished and told to mend his ways before he was sent back.

Six weeks later he was home for Christmas, a very happy one, for his sister Peg was there. She had been sent from Ireland to a boarding school in Clerkenwell. She was in her ninth year and her parents could not let her run wild in Ireland any longer in an era when fourteen was a marriageable age. As Mrs Pepys, with her acknowledged good French breeding – and socially, her husband's superior – was in every way a suitable chaperone for Peg, this was arranged. The Pepys together with the admiral and William took Peg for outings from her school. One Sunday at the end of September was a special event, for the admiral had his brother George with him, safe at last. After church they all returned to supper with the Penns and Pepys notes that Penn's 'brother speaks Spanish very well, and he is a merry man'. Those few words reveal George Penn's character like a searchlight. He was sixty-one and still suffering from his tortures: thanks to the admiral's diplomacy, his brother was safely home and was now interesting the king in his wrongs. Hope was stirring in the victim's heart at last.

The following Christmas passed as usual, but as George was not being mentioned by Pepys as present, it is assumed he had gone on a merchant voyage. The Penns and Pepys went to the theatre on New Year's Day, and returned home in a hired coach, but when they sat down to cards William found he had left his sword in the coach. He tore down the streets until he found the coach and got his sword back. He always wore it. But despite his son's courtier-like dress, the admiral realised his son could not feel happy at Oxford after his severe reprimands and thought of removing him to Cambridge. He had more sympathy with his son than he let the young man know. For years he himself had worshipped his Maker on the tossing sea, under the wide sky with never a surplice in sight, so the argument to him was technical rather than moral. He asked Pepys' advice about a change to Cambridge. But by the time Pepys had written it was too late. William was called before the Chancellor and sent down for good.

William's belief that every man should worship God in his own way was dangerous; for the Cavalier Parliament ordered that dissenters be jailed or sent into slavery for not using the Prayer Book. William was not yet a Quaker, but he already held to their tenet that it was wrong to do hat honours, that is, to doff one's hat in the presence of anyone save at the name or thought of the Creator. William accompanied his father to Court from time to time. One day, the young man found himself alone with his sovereign at some distance from others, and spoke to him without doffing his hat. Whereupon Charles, who had a delightful wit, immediately took off his own hat.

'Sire, why dost thou remove thy hat?' enquired William.

'Because in the presence of the king it is customary for one man only to wear his hat,' replied the king with a smile. The story went round London like wildfire, and the admiral was justifiably furious, but the king, who was truly fond of the lad, was merely amused.

There are many accounts of what followed. Some state that the admiral thrashed his son. Others that he took him to an Inn and knelt in the prayer, 'Dear Lord, turn my son from his Quaker ways.' William tried to throw himself out of the window, but a member of the Navy Board, passing by, came in and pacified them.

Some weeks later in the course of his normal duties the admiral discovered what troubled William's mind. At Portsmouth he was handed a packet of letters, one which proved William had been in constant correspondence with Dr Owen from the day he was sent down. Penn was on duty at Portsmouth on the king's betrothal to Catherine of Braganza, whose dowry offered England more than did any of her competitors. She brought Tangier and Bombay. Books on the island of Madeira claim that England was given the choice of Madeira, or of Bombay. England wisely chose the latter and so obtained its first enduring possession in India. It was the supremacy of the English navy at sea which had lured so many countries to offer a queen to Charles II. Lawson was sent with the fleet to fetch the young girl to England. On such an occasion everything came under the purview of the admiral and general at sea, Sir William Penn. He had inspected the ships before they sailed, then ridden down to Portsmouth to see all was in readiness for the reception of the future queen. On Sunday morning Penn was first 'to wait on my Lord Steward to church', the Duke of Ormonde now being steward of the king's household.

But despite the comfort of Ormonde's presence, Penn was so upset by Dr Owen's letter that he showed it to Pepys, whom he trusted as an intimate friend. When Penn returned home, he faced his son with the letter and threw him out of the house, but soon recalled him. All this time Ormonde was his greatest friend and counsellor. He too had sons near to William's age, whom he intended to send on a grand tour to distract their minds from various English problems and widen their education. He suggested Penn send William with them and this was agreed. In addition Ormonde invited Penn to accompany him to Ireland when he went to take up his duties as Lord Lieutenant. Penn was delighted; being governor of Kinsale, he could look up his new estates.

Meanwhile the young queen arrived at Portsmouth. The king set off with Prince Rupert to tender professions of honour when she arrived. In April, 1662, Penn was sworn a member of the privy council and in this exalted capacity accompanied King Charles to Portsmouth. When at last the queen arrived there was a bonfire outside every door in London, save only that of Lady Castlemaine who vowed to give birth at Hampton Court.

No wonder Penn was happy to think his son would soon be in Europe and himself in Ireland. Midsummer week passed in preparations for both journeys. Ormonde and Penn gave a farewell dinner for their sons, who were about to depart under the leadership of the Earl of Crawford, leader of the Scottish Presbyterians, who suffered acutely under the episcopacy laws of England. With him their sons would be safe. Penn meanwhile would visit his estates at Cork and attend the provincial council of Munster; above all he visited 'his government of Kinsale' where he had the happiness of being with his dear wife and little Richard, the delicate one.

But Penn had to cut short his longed-for visit to his family. Through an almost total lack of funds, England was being disarmed in the face of growing strife with Holland which could only lead to war. Sixty-five ships had been paid off in January 1661 and now Penn had private knowledge that more were to follow. Penn returned to London to fight.

CHAPTER SEVEN

The Second Dutch War

One example of the Navy Board's difficulties is typical of the whole English navy at that date. On 27th March, 1662, the *Guernsey,* a fifth-rate small ship was owed £3,000, for the ship had not been paid since *before* the king came in, and the men of her had been forced to borrow money in order to live. They were only able to borrow money at all, through an ingenious idea hit upon by a certain Mr Holland, a naval paymaster in the time of Cromwell. He got a bill before parliament, by which all seamen could be discharged by giving them a ticket. The government then promised to pay eight per cent of each ticket to those men who would lend the seamen the value marked on the ticket 'so long as they are unpaid'. In this way a form of stock exchange was set up and London merchants were quick to see their chance of making a fortune, as poor men getting desperate were only too grateful to receive less than the value on the ticket. This gave the merchants a profitable investment. One who did this was Thomas Guy, who came from a poor family and was four years younger than Penn. Clever in finance, this son of a lighterman made a fortune in several ways and used a large part of it to build Guy's Hospital in the city near the Tower of London and the river: Penn might have been gratified to live to see the hospital completed, for he had been greatly distressed by the plan to pay seamen by ticket when it was first devised: the good that came of it would have surprised him.

The Navy Board was also responsible for building merchant ships and boats, for in time of war the mercantile marine was called to join the navy. Only two days before the discussion concerning tickets, Pepys had been worried by a demand for an estimate for boats to be built to go to Jamaica, as a result of King Charles' proclamation on 14th December previously 'For the Encouragement of Planters in His Majesty's Island of Jamaica in the West Indies'. King Charles was well aware of the value of Jamaica and knew he owed it to Penn. He determined to encourage more of his subjects to go out there to make their fortunes and his own. The terms of his proclamation were alluring. 'We being fully satisfied that our island of Jamaica, being pleasant and most fertile and situate most commodiously for Trade and Commerce, is likely to be a great benefit and advantage . . . have thought fit for encouraging our subjects . . . [to] transport themselves there . . .' The effect on the planters was salutary; not so on courtly society back home. The arrival of wealth in England's ports during the first years of Charles's reign had a most unfortunate effect on these young men, mostly landed gentry, who had followed Charles through Europe and had no means of earning a living once they returned and ceased to be mercenaries. They seized upon the idea of becoming naval officers and capturing booty of which they would get the lion's share. It was a great worry to the Navy Board who had to provide naval officers; it was a nightmare to Penn, who better than anyone else knew the consequences of untrained command in sea battles. The Duke of York equally knew the consequences. When he had gone to Portsmouth to meet the royal bride his quick, observant eye noticed the difference between professional seamen and the new captains and he told the Earl of Sandwich he 'perceived it must be the old captains that must do this business and that the new ones would spoil all.'

Pepys with his long naval experience was far more able to amass money for himself than any cavalier naval officers could do. He had begun modestly enough in 1660 by taking Captain Holland's advice at the Dog Tavern and pocketing some of the seamen's wages for himself when he went on board the *Naseby*. But by 2nd August he wrote 'so great is the present profit of this office above what it was . . . in the last king's time, there being last month two hundred bills, whereas in the last king's time it was much to have forty.'

Later there came a navy contract for masts. At that date Sir William Warren was probably the biggest timber merchant in Britain and on 10th September, 1663, Pepys was up betimes and sat all morning making a

> great contract with Sir W. Warren for 3,000£ of Masts. But good God, to see what a man might do were I a knave . . . the whole business being done by me out of office, and signed by them [the Navy Board] upon but once reading of it to them, without consultation either of quality, price, number of need of them. But I

hope my pains were such as the king hath the best bargain of masts had been bought these twenty seven years.

In this remark we meet Pepys at his best. He had made money out of giving the contract to Warren, but what bothered and infuriated him beyond all, time after time, was that Penn himself watched every detail of refitting the ships, checking quality of timber and measured the quantity. Pepys regarded it as pure interference, ignoring the fact that it was Penn and his seamen who would be going to sea in these ships and depending on the strength of the masts against gales and shots in high seas and battles.

Pepys was driven to fury when he heard that Penn was to be appointed assistant comptroller of the Navy Board to old Sir John Minnes. Had he ever been able to see the *Several Tracts relating to the Navy of England* as they were found among Sir William Penn's papers, headed with his motto DUM CLAVUM TENEAM, Pepys would have been filled with more than hatred; he would have overflowed with terror, for such total knowledge of naval misdemeanours in finance were laid bare as would have made any merchant navy adventurer bankrupt in one voyage. There was an angry board meeting in October 1663 concerning the taking of fees, but the duke must have been a tactful chairman, who wished to keep his board together in unity, for he said 'that he wished we had all made more profit than he had of our places'. After which the meeting ended.

Pepys' fortune of £7,000 was built up, not only by gifts, but from being first commissioner of Tangier and treasurer in 1665. For the tremendous English project of building the mole at Tangier in deep water to withstand the force of Atlantic gales was engineering beyond its time and so was the money which accrued from the contracts. To sailors fighting in the Mediterranean, far from home, it was a tremendous boon, to the landsman navy commissioner, a gold mine.

If Penn was paid his quarterly salary it was all he got. For economy's sake, he had to keep his family in Ireland as much as possible, and if he ever got there it was only for a brief stay. For when he was not at the Navy Board meetings, or on occasions in parliament, he was making sorties at sea because the Dutch fleet were beginning warlike manoeuvres.

* * *

Early in 1664 conversation in the coffee houses was to the effect, as

Pepys remarked that 'the trade of the world is too little for us two, therefore one must down'. Although war between England and Holland was not declared until March 1665, hostilities had existed between Dutch settlers and English merchants as early as February 1664 and in May of that year Sir William Penn was ordered to Portsmouth to see to the hasty fitting out of the ships.

It did not surprise him, he had already written to his wife in Ireland and his son in France to make all haste to return to England. William was no longer at the court of King Louis, where he had first gone, for he had asked to go to study at the famous College of Saumur under the great philosopher, Amyraut. Until his death it was the fashion for English Protestant families of note to send their boys there. One member of the Vane family, if not Henry Vane himself, was educated there. It meant hard work for the lectures were in French. William arrived at Harwich in August, the same month that his mother and Richard arrived from Ireland. Penn was in London to greet them all, for he had been recalled from Portsmouth after being only one month there: it was indeed a privilege for Penn to be called to London to meet Ormonde on business connected with the family's Irish estates. But this call also proved to be tragically most timely. Brother George, who had suffered so terribly under the Spanish Inquisition, had been living near to Penn in London and the king had recently appointed him as resident envoy at the king of Spain's court, 'with commands that he should insist upon satisfaction from that king, for his sufferings, loss and damage..' When Penn was in Portsmouth, Captain George was waiting to be sufficiently recovered to take up his appointment. But hardly had Penn returned, before Pepys was awakened in the night with knocking at his neighbour's door. 'And what was it but people's running up and down to bring him word that his brother, Captain Penn, who hath a great while been sick, is dead?' Penn's grief was all the greater since he had believed he might soon see his brother restored to his former fortune, if not to his original health. But George's age, sixty-three years, prevented it.

The funeral took place two nights following and the cortège consisted of the officers of the Navy Board, together with Sir William Penn and the servants of the house. He was buried under the communion table in the chancel of St Olave's, the Navy Board church. It was kept strictly private and, according to the fashion for persons of rank, he was buried at night.

In his brother's will, Penn was the sole heir. Characteristically he did not give up the battle his brother had not lived to fight. Penn felt the cruelties suffered were unforgiveable, so that the international lawsuit continued as long as Penn lived, and when he died his son took it up with Queen Anne during the negotiations for peace at Utrecht.

His brother's death, sixteen days before his own family set foot on English soil, saddened the family reunion. However one fact brought joy. William had apparently lost his dangerous unfashionable ideas. All went well at court too, where William's manners were those of a perfect courtier. The king liked him and courtiers noted that his French was impeccable while his pantaloons gave an excellent impression. The admiral now began to plan William's future as an ambassador and entered him in Lincoln's Inn, one of the great law schools. He had a good brain and his memory was almost photographic when it came to learning Coke's *Institute of Law*. This was to save him from prison and establish the right of trial by jury in days to come. Now his father was certain that his son was not to become a 'tarpaulin' like himself. Penn would wryly recall the dinner party arranged to discuss how best to make the calling of the navy seem a suitable profession for young noblemen and gentlemen and going to sea as honourable a service as a land war. All this seems particularly strange in an island race whose fortunes depended increasingly on overseas trade, and the elimination of Dutch rivalry.

Pepys's jealousy of Penn never let him forget his own superiority as a graduate of Magdalene College, Cambridge, but, above all, as the second Dutch war now loomed, he loved to reiterate his insulting characterisation of Lady Penn: 'A well-looking, fat, short old Dutchwoman but one that hath been pretty handsome; and is now very discreet and I believe hath more wit than her husband.' Margaret had no active Dutch connexions. The implied slur on Penn's loyalty was misplaced.

* * *

Commercial rivalry was the cause of the Second Dutch War. This rivalry extended from India to West Africa and from the West Indies to the Atlantic shores of America. In the four years of peace between the two countries, men at the court of Charles II, from the Duke of York downwards, took almost as great an interest in overseas enterprises as courtiers had done in the days of Queen Elizabeth I. In February 1664 the Dutch entered the English factory at Surat, two hundred miles north of Bombay, beating up the men there and raising the Dutch flag. In parliament, resolutions were passed demanding the king to exact right for the wrong done. The Dutch also stirred up the native populations to drive the English from their lands in Africa and from their recently acquired land round Bombay, the queen's dowry.

Officially, the countries were still at peace when the English landed a force in America in May 1664 to capture New Amsterdam and New Netherlands, which they promptly renamed New York. This squadron was sent out by the Duke of York who had lost money when the Dutch captured ships belonging to the Royal West African Company. There was no land fighting in America. The Dutch had only a small number of settlers among the comparatively populous English. The expedition would certainly have appealed to Penn, and considering how much its success would mean to the duke and his great belief in Penn's capabilities, it is probable that Penn conducted this important squadron.

Charles II finally declared war in March 1665; a war the Duke of York and Penn had been preparing for nearly a year, ever since both houses attended the king to demand the curtailment of the activities of the Dutch. The duke lost no time. He accompanied the king to Chatham, taking with him the admiral on whom he so greatly relied, together with a 'great crew' of navy men, to examine and hurry on the preparations.

Each side had one advantage which the other side had not got. Finance is the sinews of war and the resources of the republic were much sounder than those of the British crown. The Dutch had amassed so much wealth that Holland could borrow all the money needed at four per cent interest, while England, if she could find anyone to lend money at all, had to pay at least eight per cent interest. On the other hand the English ships fought together as a navy. Penn had instituted this from his first command in Ireland and called his captains together to discuss battle procedure with them. The Dutch, meanwhile, were administered by five independant admiralty boards, of Rotterdam, Amsterdam, Zeeland, Friesland, and the North Quarter. It was a system infinitely more divisive than the personal bickerings of the Navy Board, who were totally united as Englishmen once war began.

Partly as a result of this superior English organisation, and partly because of Penn's personal vigilance, England was better equipped for the forthcoming war than her financial stringency and her traditional unreadiness might lead one to expect. Penn's commitment was concentrated to particular effect in two areas: the morale and welfare of the service, and the quality and design of the ships. There was little that could be done to reduce an ordinary sailor's vulnerability in battle; while an admiral could grace his bridge in full knightly panoply of traditional armour, ratings had to go barefoot up and down the rigging for their own safety. Shots could not be deflected, nor blows averted. But Penn did realise that the care of the wounded could be improved, and created commissioners for the care of the sick and wounded, county by county. Evelyn, the diarist, served for Kent and Sussex. Penn also alerted the hospitals of St Thomas and St Bartholomew in London to be ready for the reception of wounded sailors. Meanwhile, in the months of the approach of war, Penn had spent much time in the dockyards with Commissioner Pett, devising detailed improvements to the fleet, resolving small but vital problems, like the inflow of water during manoeuvres that would cause the nethermost of a first-rate ship's four tiers of guns to plunge beneath the waves. By the time war broke out, it is probably fair to say that, technically and in terms of morale, the fleet had never been in better shape.

The solicitude for detail that made Penn so effective in these fields is demonstrated by the code he issued just a fortnight after he had been given his instructions by the Lord High Admiral at Portsmouth. Penn specified just what he wanted of his serving captains in these *Duties of a Commander at Sea, 1664, Instructions by Sir W. Penn.* They were written in Penn's own hand and went into every possible detail of a commander's duties such as:

> Before the ship goes to sea he appoints a sufficient number of men to manage the great guns . . . sails . . . and small shot . . . that on any occasion each man may perfectly know his duty by causing a table fairly written, to be hung in the steerage containing all men's names and respective quarters, to which gun they are attached with a boy, to serve them with powder . . . He shall not count any man an able seaman who hath not served at sea for seven years at least . . .'

The duke had decided that the English fleet should consist of three squadrons, to be commanded by himself, Prince Rupert and Lord Sandwich; from which arrangement the two last, who were land-admirals, had concluded that Penn would have no concern in this fleet. Neither the duke nor Rupert, nor Sandwich had ever been engaged in an encounter of fleets. The duke, though he had greatly distinguished himself on land under Marshal Turenne, had never witnessed a fight at sea. Rupert with his small, predatory squadron had been beaten by Blake in 1650 and chased round the Mediterranean by Penn; and, though he was well practised in high-sea piracy, was wholly a stranger to naval war. He, also, was only a soldier. Penn alone, of the four, was familiar with all these things. By the duke's unexpected announcement, that he would take Penn with him into his own ship, Rupert and Sandwich at once discovered, that they would be really and practically under Penn's command. On 30th November, 1664, the Lord High Admiral ordered Penn to shift his flag from the *James* to the first rate, *Royal Charles,* the duke's own ship. Penn was named as the Great Captain Commander, with his trusted John Harman as captain of the flagship. Harman had served under Penn in the Mediterranean and had carried his dispatches after the defeat of the Dutch in 1652.

When Prince Rupert heard that Penn was actually on board the *Royal Charles* and therefore in real command of the whole fleet, he swore an oath that Penn should never go to sea again.

* * *

Penn's compassion and care had often been demonstrated before. What had previously gone unremarked was his great stature as a tactical innovator. As we have seen, he had begun to evolve new tactical disciplines for fighting ships from his earliest years in command. At his first great victory over Tromp, in February, 1653, he had launched a rapier-like thrust at the centre of the enemy's line, maximising the fire-power of his own ships. Now, in the Second Dutch War, exploiting his effective position of supreme command, he was to impose this new method throughout the fleet.

The *Intelligencer* of 5th June was correct in its deduction that as the sound of the guns grew further and further off, his Majesty's navy was driving the Dutch before them. That is exactly what happened, as Penn's plan was to force the whole of the enemy fleet into the harbour mouth of the Texel and blockade them there. The English fleet knew what to do, for they had been disciplined and fully briefed on 18th April by the issue of *The Duke of York's Instructions for better fighting* which had been signed and drawn up in Penn's own hand.

The basic truth which Penn taught in these instructions was the one he had previously made plain to his commanders en route to the West Indies, 'Time spent in reconnaisance is seldom wasted.' Instruction No. 1 read: 'Upon discovery of a fleet . . . one frigate out of each squadron is to make sail and stand with them so nigh as conveniently may, the better to get the knowledge of what they are . . . and conclude on the report they are to give to their respective squadrons and commanders-in-chief.'

This was an innovation of great importance for it forged the English ships into one fighting unit out of merchant navy and regular navy men. The second point Penn insisted on was that each ship had its own place in its respective squadron.

The third article of the *Duke of York's Instructions* written by Penn himself and carried out by him to the letter in the battle of Lowestoft, was the most important of all. It read

> In case the enemy have the wind of the admiral and fleet, and they have sea-room enough, they are to keep the wind as close as they can lie, until they see an opportunity by gaining their wakes, to divide the enemy's fleet and if the van of his Majesty's fleet find they have the wake of any considerable part of them, they are to tack, stand in and strive to divide the enemy's body: . . . that squadron that shall pass first to windward is to bear down on those ships to leeward of them . . . the middle squadron is to keep her wind and the last squadron is to second . . . and both squadrons are to do their utmost to assist the first squadron that divided the enemy's fleet.

Penn signalled. All ships to sail in line, all squadrons to tack simultaneously. Then he sailed the *Royal Charles* to the head of the line and led towards the centre of the Dutch line, where Obdam, with whom he was determined 'to have a bout' was in command. But he had to do this without the help of the brave sailor Sandwich, for as Penn stood on the forecastle watching through his glass he saw that the *Royal Oak* was not doing as well as usual, and a small pinnace was approaching. It brought the bad news that Lawson, wounded through the knee could not stand up on deck to command,. Penn then sent Captain Jordan to the *Royal Oak* 'where he did excellent service'.

Penn continued to lead the line towards the first Dutch squadron where the Lord of Obdam commanded the foe. Penn put up a 'press of sail' until the *Royal Charles* and the *Eendracht* were touching each other.

There is a wonderful Dutch oil painting in the Maritime Museum at Greenwich of the two ships with their prows touching. This painting gives a truer idea of the dangers, courage and horrors of fighting than a whole book could do.

A shot from the *Royal Charles* hit the *Eendracht* in the powder room. The ship blew up, covering the *Royal Charles* with smoke and burning débris. Obdam was killed instantly, Penn escaped unhurt, just as he escaped in the first Dutch war when a shot from his ship killed Tromp.

As soon as the *Eendracht* sank, the Dutch fleet turned into 'a Rowte' and fled towards the safety of the Texel. But the victory masked a tragedy of some importance for the English because three cavalier officers standing together on deck on the *Royal Charles* were killed instantly by the one and same cannon ball. They were the Earl of Falmouth, Lord Muskerry and Mr Boyle, second son of the Boyle family, close friends of Penn from early Irish days. The death of these three cavaliers completely shook the already low morale of the court favourites whose presence on board had greatly hindered, not helped, the old tarpaulins. The fact that Falmouth's death would mean great grief to His Majesty, who was fond of him, gave strength to the plan they now formulated.

When night fell, the English were still in hot pursuit of the Dutch who were flying in total disorder to the Texel, the condition of most of the ships being beyond fighting, masts down, sails burned. That night of 5th June, when the duke and Penn saw the 'confused rowte' of the fleeing enemy, they were certain victory was won. It only meant continuing in full sail, to catch and destroy the poor remainder as they drove them into the Texel. So the two friends and commanders retired to rest, but not before Penn had given the command, strongly supported by the duke, that the fleet was to follow the Dutch with all possible haste to the Dutch coast and destroy the remainder before they could enter the Texel. Penn then went to his cabin. He was hardly able to stand from the agony of gout. He had directed the battle from three in the morning until ten that night, fully clad in a suit of armour which today hangs in the church of St Mary Redcliffe, Bristol – helmet, visor, breast plate, cuisses down to his feet. One of the cavalier gentlemen of the bedchamber waited until he could make sure that both Penn and the duke were sound asleep and reported to Lord Brounckner. Brounckner then went to Captain Harman and gave him orders in the duke's name, that all sails must be slackened. Such an order greatly surprised Harman, who knew Penn far too well to understand it. He hesitated, but naval discipline was strict. To question would have been insubordination if not mutiny. Harman gave the orders to slacken sail. Men ran up the rigging, the signal was hoisted and so the gap widened increasingly between the English and the fleeing Dutch.

But the plotters were quick to act before dawn broke. They passed the order to Harman to speed sail as before, so that when the Duke and Penn appeared on deck after dawn, the *Royal Charles* was in full sail, but the Dutch were no longer in sight. Had Penn's orders been carried out there would have been no Dutch fleet at all, only a few shattered remains.

However, the next day, when the Duke of Albemarle (the grand new title of George Monck) read Coventry's letter, he found himself overflowing with joy. Pepys captures his response 'a great victory, never known in the world. They are all fled, forty-three got into the Texel, we in pursuit of the rest.' Pepys then went to Lady Penn's, 'where they are all joyed and not a little puffed up at the good success of their father . . . had a great bonfire at the gate . . . good service is said to have been done by him.' The magnitude of the victory is suggested by figures compiled by Sir William Coventry at the end of the war. Of forty-three English ships' captains killed in the course of conflict, only five fell that day under Penn's command off Lowestoft.

The *Royal Charles* put in on 16th June and the duke called the Navy Board to attend him the same afternoon in Whitehall, where the court was full of 'the duke and his courtiers returned from sea, lusty and ruddy being in the sun'. However, the news of Sir John Lawson was disquieting. He was in hospital in Greenwich, where Penn visited him when he left Whitehall. The Lord Treasurer had gone out of town for fear of the bubonic plague: one seventh of London's population was killed by it. But Penn looked well, according to Pepys, who saw him at the Navy Board on the 16th: 'I am gladder to see him than otherwise I should be, because my hearing so well of him for his serviceableness in this late, great action.'

Penn must have indeed looked well after his return from victory to hear that a thanksgiving day of victory had been ordered by parliament to take place in London and Westminster on Tuesday, 20th June. One thing only happened to cast a cloud over his happiness: the death of Sir

John Lawson; his body was accompanied by the principal officers and commissioners of the navy to St Dunstan's at night, as was customary for those of high rank. But Penn's religious instincts tempered his sense of loss and made him thank God he had been able to serve his country with success.

Penn's official report submitted to the government on 8th June was afterwards published in the *Intelligencer.* Effectively describing Penn's tactical system in action, it read:

> *A summary narration of the signal victory which it pleased Almighty God to bestow upon his Majesty's navy, under the Command of H.R.H. the Duke of York, against the Dutch fleet of the State of the United Netherlands, on 3rd June, 1665 . . .* June 2nd we followed till night . . . H.R.H. made his sign for tacking to keep the wind . . . in the third brunt, we engaged in a line but they still bore off . . . which way of fighting seemed tedious to us, so about one of the clock we passed so near the middle of them that we divided their fleet . . . Opdam's ship was blown up so we fell pell-mell in with them . . . God hath been pleased to give a great victory, the enemy being driven into the Texel as far as draught of water would permit.

Nowhere in the report does he use the first person; all we learn about Penn is to be inferred from what later historians discovered: the anonymous 'we', 'us' and denoted none, was Penn himself. Two very distinguished modern historians – C. V. Wedgwood and Richard Ollard – have said such an account was far too modest. Penn could have claimed the victory. A. W. G. Pearsall writes that 'much of the credit for the victory of Lowestoft must go to him.' But all contemporary opinion gave the honour to the duke. Yet the king and duke knew how much credit was due to Penn for the victory, for in 1680, ten years after Penn's death, they gave the tract of territory in America to his son William in 'the memory and merit of Sir William Penn . . . particularly his conduct, courage and discretion under our dearest brother the Duke of York against the Dutch fleet commanded by heer Van Obdam in 1665'. Yet apart from a mention by Bishop Parker in the *History of his own Times* it was not until a textbook of 1883, that Penn's role was adequately celebrated by his own countrymen. As the authors of the *Modern Universal History* say, 'in 1665 Sir William Penn was appointed to command the English Fleet under the Duke of York and it was universally thought that the laurels which H.R.H. won in the fighting were chiefly owing to the great abilities of Sir William Penn, the seaman.''

The paucity of these facts, together with the political situation of the day, meant that it was left to a foreign historian, the famous Frenchman Paul Hoste, Professor of Mathematics in the Royal Seminary of Toulon, to give Penn his true position as one of the greatest of admirals. In 1697 he published *L'Art des armées navales,* later translated as *Naval Evolution, or a System of Sea-Discipline.* He made a special study of winds on waves and the sails of ships in naval manoeuvres. He proceeded to give examples from famous naval battles throughout history, including the defeat of the Armada.

In the second part of the treatise, Hoste declared that he found Penn's tactics revolutionary. Never before had any commander used the like in naval warfare, until Penn fought his two battles off the Texel, off Port Talbot (1653) and off Falmouth (1655). Before then, opposing naval forces had always sailed abreast, their keels parallel, or in an arc, and each vessel then fought in individual combat. Hoste declared Penn to be the first sea-captain to instruct his ships to sail in line through the centre of the opposing line and only as they sailed behind the enemy line, were they to sail in either direction, and fall into individual combat. In this way, the line of ships cutting through the enemy's centre fired its broadsides from both sides of its decks, so doubling its fire against the enemy. Written in French, the book was translated into English in 1762 by Christopher O'Bryen, a lieutenant in the Royal Navy.

Hoste had spent twelve years at sea and was himself an enemy subject, so his study was both informed and dispassionate. The book was adopted as a training book. After the sale of commissions was made illegal to those who had not passed examinations, this book had to be studied. Nelson would have to study it and he used Penn's tactics in a modified form against the astonished French at Trafalgar. Such immitation was fit tribute, for Penn anticipated Nelson in other ways too. In tactics and technique, in his struggle against graft and abuse, in his compassion for the men, in his attention to morale, in his insistence on a command of practical seamanship as the key to victory, and, above all, in his habit of winning battles, Penn had emerged, by the time of the second Dutch war, as one of the great makers – and makers secure – of the English naval tradition.

* * *

Immediately after the victory, the fleet came into the river to be repaired for the sequel to the summer's expedition. Penn was anxious to take to sea again and on 10th June letters emerged from the *Royal Charles* saying, 'Our generals remain on board using all possible diligence to repair the fleet, which will in a few days be in condition to take to sea again.'

Penn waited for orders to sail but two weeks elapsed and no such orders came. Meanwhile, the Dutch, who were at first so badly demoralised by their defeat that they had no thought of taking the offensive, began to realise, when 1st July passed without any English action, that the English command was inexplicably hamstrung. They worked wonders repairing their shattered ships and morale. Their problem was to find a commander-in-chief, now Tromp was dead and De Ruyter heading a rich treasure fleet somewhere in mid-Atlantic.

This news had considerable effect on the cavalier party which dominated parliament and those cavalier seamen who had bought commissions solely in the hope of the prize money to be gained. But after Lowestoft they had sampled their fill. They worked on Charles to end the war and put the life of his brother, the Lord High Admiral, out of danger. To all of which Charles agreed, though he would not agree to the demands of Prince Rupert that he should now command the whole fleet in lieu of Penn, nor would he make him Lord High Admiral, for both York and Coventry regarded Rupert in command as a danger to be avoided at all costs. Charles compromised by putting the fleet under the Earl of Sandwich, with Sir William Penn as Admiral of the White and Sir Thomas Allen as Admiral of the Blue. For his safety from both the sea and the plague, the duke was sent to York to take charge of the defences.

Meanwhile Penn continued to press hard that the fleet should quickly refit and return at once to the Texel and 'finish the job' by finally destroying the Dutch fleet before it could come out again. Pepys knew this and may have been present at Navy Board meetings when the plan was being discussed. For months later, on 16th October, Penn's advice having been ignored, Pepys wrote that at dinner at the Tower of London with Albemarle and the duchess, much of the talk was of the Dutch coming ashore and stealing sheep and the blame being laid on the commanders of the English navy: 'How much better if the Duke of York's advice had been taken, for the fleet to have gone presently [immediately] out.' But the king completely ignored the advice and sent the fleet to the defensive position of Sole-Bay where it had to stay until news came that the rich East India fleet was coming round Scotland. Penn was the first to sail. But aided by misty weather, De Ruyter slipped into the Ems with a number of prizes. The two fleets returned to the old days of merchant ship marauding, so when at last the English returned with very rich prizes about £400,000 the Navy Board was certainly cheered. Sandwich complained that Penn had gone to sea before him, but it did nothing for Sandwich's reputation. For he was in trouble over money. On his return with his rich prizes he had allowed his seamen the plunder of all goods lying open between decks. This was both customary and legal. But officers, by law, were prohibited from 'breaking bulk', that is opening the holds and helping themselves to bonded cargo. Sandwich, in agreement with some of his flag officers though in opposition to Penn and some others, broke bulk and sent some of the goods away by sea. Pepys borrowed money to buy himself £1,000 of goods. But customs officers were quick to follow it up, and, although Pepys cleverly disentangled himself, the scandal concerning Sandwich grew. There was talk of impeachment. The king did not relish such an action against his commander-in-chief so he sent him to Madrid as ambassador, hoping that during his absence the scandal would be forgotten. It was temporarily effaced. But scandals scotched, not killed, have remarkable powers of recovery. This one, as we shall see, was to re-emerge later with terrible destructive force.

The king's next act was to call parliament on 30th September to pass several bills; then he prorouged them. The Commons were generous to the king over the war, for one bill passed gave him £2,500,000 to be raised in three years for the maintenance of the Dutch war. Yet the terrible plague which was fast emptying the city seems not have been discussed. With Sandwich a failure and sent to Madrid, who was to command the navy? Penn was the duke's choice but that was impossible in view of the strength of cavalier support for Rupert. The king made Rupert and Monck joint commanders. Reluctantly the duke agreed that the only naval man who could snatch victory out of the Dutch, must stay on shore as a commissioner of the Navy Board, refitting, repairing, building ships. It was probably one of the bitterest moments of Penn's life. His consolation was the presence of his wife and family and the fact that William did not flee London from the plague, but daily attended the law lectures at Lincoln's Inn. For London had seen nothing like the Great Plague since the Black Death. The Navy Board remained in London long after businesses had closed down, their companions being those who had nowhere else to go. On 28th July the king ordered the Navy Board to remove to the Palace of Greenwich. In the first week in September Penn insisted that his wife and family must be lodged at Woolwich. It was easy for Penn to visit his family going down there by river. Like his father, however, William stayed on and his daily walk through the city had a strong effect on him. He wrote that it revived his sense of 'the Vanity of this world and the Irreligiousness of the Religious of it'.

CHAPTER EIGHT

'The Fittest Man' Ashore

Early in January 1666, France, in the person of King Louis himself, declared war on England. The Danes quickly followed suit, rightly angered at Sandwich having ordered a squadron to attack all the Dutch merchant ships lying in Bergen, though the governor had told him he must not bring in more than five ships of war. Discreditable negotiations between the two governments failed and this blow to Sandwich caused great rejoicing among the Dutch. The result was a greatly increased work load at the already fully employed Navy Board. There was also a disastrous need of money to carry out what had suddenly become a new necessity – the defence of England. Nor could it have come at a worse time, for though the plague was abating, London was decimated. Meanwhile the Great Captain Commander, Admiral and General at Sea, Sir William Penn, struggled with sterile problems of administration, in impotent exclusion from command. While the enemy gathered at sea, the ablest man in England stayed ashore.

Visits to different ports meant that Penn's presence at the Navy Board could never be predicted either there or at home, Pepys' writes on 11th January, 1666 to remind us of a widening of Penn's family circle: 'All of us by invitation to Sir W Penn's and much company, among others the Lieutenant of the Tower and Dr Whistler and his [prospective] son-in-law Lower, servant to Mrs Margaret Penn.' Anthony Lowther of Mask, Cleaveland, was the step-son of Dr Whistler and came from a very substantial Yorkshire family. He was nine years older than Peg, but it is more than possible that the two families had long known each other through Bristol trade with the famous Yorkshire Carpet Weavers. Penn now had to find a daughter's dowry and discussed this with Pepys. But he had not got Pepys' manner of raising cash. However, Penn knew how to direct shrewd questions at Pepys regarding the finances of the fleet for the new campaign, for it was calculated that there was but £1,500,000 to answer expenses and debts of £2,300,000. It came as a nasty shock because the English attempts to form a continental coalition against the Dutch had failed. The only ruler they could persuade to join them was that 'fire eating prelate' the Prince-bishop of Münster, and his invasion of Gelderland was quickly stopped by the French. England was alone. Yet despite the financial difficulties which hampered Penn and the Navy Board they achieved the miracle of having some seventy sail ready in the Downs by the end of May. This was one week before de Ruyter could put to sea from the Texel, though he had greatly superior Dutch finances behind his fleet.

Prince Rupert and Monck now exercised joint command for the new campaign and their flag flew in the *Royal Charles*. Monck intended to proceed to the Downs and as a distinguished soldier demonstrate to the country the great inferiority of the Dutch at sea (as well as of English seamen). But reports that a French fleet from Toulon was on its way, triggered off a plan to divide the fleet, one to meet the French, the other to face the large Dutch fleet under De Ruyter. Had Penn been in command this would not have happened. He never allowed the fleet to be divided. But Penn was not in command; he was actively engaged in the dockyards ordering the building of ships and their repair. Monck was uneasy and wrote to the king who replied by suggesting he change his station for the Gunfleet, 'where the great ships remaining may come to join with you and you cannot be forced to do anything but what you please, which in the Downes you cannot.'

Finally Rupert's squadron was seen and Monck sailed to meet the reinforcements on a course 'which led him over one end of the Galloper Sands'. A tragedy ensued. The *Royal Prince* 92 brass guns, the finest ship in the English fleet, stuck fast and was captured. De Ruyter had her crew taken off, Sir George Ayscue was made prisoner and the ship burnt. The following three days of action were equally disastrous; so the General made sign to retreat.

Both sides were severely shattered. The Dutch took 1,800 prisoners, the English took none. Penn's old ship, the *Swiftsure* was captured as was the *Essex*. Monck laid all the blame on his officers. Penn wrote to his son in Ireland, 'I have been from my house almost three weeks, cast upon the hardest work of the shattered fleet . . . I could send you particulars of the last battle, but none so unfit, which makes me silent.' To Pepys, however, he unburdened: the fleet should not have engaged; indeed, the Downs station should not have been left; the English ships were too low in the water to fire their lower tiers of guns; 'we must not desert ships of our own in distress', ships 'with small disabling,' must make do and fight on; above all, 'we must fight in a line, whereas we fight promiscuously, to our utter and demonstrable ruin'. As for the command,

> He told me that our very commanders, nay our very flag-officers, do stand in need of exercizing among themselfs and discoursing the business of commanding a fleet – he telling me that even one of our flag-men in the fleet did not know which tacke lost the wind or which kept it in the last engagement.

The Dutch were at sea again by 26th June, with 2,700 soldiers on board ready to invade England. But Penn knew that Sheerness was the key to the coastal defences and he had spent much time there organising its defence. De Ruyter soon found this out and sent his soldiers home. The Dutch fleet then cruised off the Naze in order to blockade the English coast, but the English were ready for action.

News spread quickly and made the name of Admiral Penn a name to be conjured with. The king and the Duke of York showed their confidence in him openly. The duke wrote to Penn on 20th July giving him 'full power and authority to give such orders as shall seem to you most conducible to his Majesty's service; willing and requiring all his majesty's officers, ships and yards, to follow such orders as you shall send them as they will answer to the contrary.' This made Penn the chief naval commissioner. So though the duke had not been able to give Penn the command of the fleet, he gave him the power to order any of the ships to return to wherever he chose to send them in the battle about to begin.

An entry in Pepys's *Diary* reminds one that the English character changes very little in danger, for on their way from seeing the Duke of York at St James's, Penn and Pepys had been ordered to stop at Lely's studio 'for Penn to have a time appointed when to be drawn among other commanders of flags in the last year's fight.' Drake had paused similarly, on a comparable occasion, for a famous game of bowls.

At last Rupert and Monck had learned they must keep their ships together and the main Dutch fleet made for home. But the English followed up their victory in a most discreditable manner, 'Holmes's Bonfire' was a lasting disgrace to the English navy. After finding fifty sail in the harbour of the Vly, all loaded merchantmen of great worth, the English sent in 1,500 men and fireboats and burnt them all. Then they pillaged the neat town of Terschelling and burnt all of it. It was not only the Dutch, but the English Calvinists who saw God's retribution in the Fire of London two months later. The English meanwhile, regarded the sack of Terschelling as a providential proof of victory and gave thanksgiving services and parties to celebrate. Pepys records supper parties, Lady Penn and Peg dancing till three in the morning. Sir William Penn is never mentioned for he was on war duty at Sheerness. He got back on 22nd August when he made it clear he did not approve of the English marines burning and pillaging the prosperous town and injuring women and children.

Ten days after Penn was made chief naval commissioner the Fire of London started. It began near Fish Street, close to London Bridge, and in four days reduced the whole city to ashes from the Tower of London to the Temple. Penn had the idea of blowing up houses to make a fire gap and the duke had long since trained a band of marines who were called into action pulling down houses to make fire gaps and helping the homeless to boats on the river and safety. Fortunately the flames stopped at the base of Tower Hill, which like the Tower itself, remained unscathed, as did the Navy office and the houses in Navy Gardens. But at the west gate of the city, or the Ludgate, the church of St Martin-Within-Ludgate, where Penn was married, was burned to ashes. Fortunately the custom of the time was to copy all marriages within the city walls into leather volumes kept in the vaults of the Guildhall, and this preserved the record of event for posterity. Living on the hill above the river with a clear road to Wanstead it took only a short time for Penn to send his family to safety.

The tragedy of the Fire was but a spark in the furnace of trouble caused by the state of naval finances, non-payment of poor sailors, merchants, victuallers and honest officers such as Penn, who never once received his salary of one thousand pounds a year. Parliament was forced to pay attention. On 28th August Pepys wrote of *A letter from the Generals to the king,* 'a most scurvy letter reflecting upon Sir W. Coventry and me for my accounts'. The generals were attempting to fasten their ill success at sea upon the Navy Office. Penn was sent to report on the state of the navy and Pepys called to a cabinet meeting where he made a good speech disclosing the ill state of the navy and the greatness of its debts. He writes, 'I had no sooner done but Prince

Rupert rose and told the king in great heat that whatever the gentleman had said, he had brought home his fleet in as good condition as any fleet was brought home. He repeated what he had said, but, after a long silence, nobody seconded the Prince. We withdrew.' It drove the prince to the edge of madness; no power on earth now would be able to stop his revenge.

Meanwhile William carried on his father's business in Ireland. The admiral now called him home in time for Peg's marriage. Peg or Margaret Penn married Anthony Lowther on Valentine's Day, 1667, at the family church of St Olave's, Hart Street, only the family being present. Eight days later they gave a dinner and presented all the guests with 'favours' to put in their hats to wear when they appeared at court later in the day. For her parents had to take the bride to be presented to their Majesties once more, on the occasion of her marriage, and the wedding guests would accompany them. On this great occasion 'Peg was adorned with jewels fit for a duchess'. On 1st May surprise followed surprise, 'for in addition to seeing her in a coach that was finer than the king's, Peg Lowther appeared in a dress and jewels which were like those of a duchess'.

* * *

As C. V. Wedgwood has written, 'The catastrophe of the Medway might have been avoided if the Pepys' Navy Board colleagues had taken notice of Admiral Penn's warnings.'

In June 1667 the Dutch sailed up the Medway and burned our ships where they lay. It was the greatest disgrace in our proud maritime history. During the winter season of 1666-67 when ships were being prepared for the summer campaign against the Dutch, the Duke of York voiced Penn's suggestions to the king and pressed them most strongly. If there must be war, attack was the surest form of defence. In the *Life of the Duke of York,* written by himself, the duke wrote that the king had been persuaded by Monck and others to lay up first and second-class ships altogether, and fight only a defensive war. The duke wrote that he most strongly opposed this, but he was over-ruled.
No stronger proof than his own word is needed.

Neither Penn nor the duke wanted war for the sake of war, but until the Dutch signed a peace treaty, England must continue to prepare to defend herself. Information arrived weekly that the Dutch fleet, hidden in the Texel, was working hard to restore its former efficiency and if the Dutch did want peace it would be peace on their own terms. In fact both countries wanted peace, though probably England more than Holland. The sufferings of the plague followed by the Great Fire of London had caused terrible financial losses and though parliament voted more money the bill was not passed until January 1667. Meanwhile, starving men deserted; ships mutinied; men of all ranks stole whenever possible, if not on the enormous scale of Pepys. Merchants were becoming difficult over lending money and the City was loath to oblige further.

But the king firmly believed that the Dutch were anxious for peace in order to resume their profitable overseas trade. He had, moreover, made a secret treaty with Louis XIV who stated he would give no help to the United provinces and in May would attack the Spanish-held Netherlands. So the king was adamant against preparing the fleet as formerly. Coventry said, 'The English must have peace for no fleet could be fitted out.' They failed to grasp the effect of Holmes's Bonfire and the furious longing for revenge of Johan de Witt, the Dutch supremo.

On 6th March the Duke of York summoned the Navy Board to inform them of the plans already known to Penn's dismay. 'The duke declared his expectation of the enemy's blocking us up in the river, so directed we send away all ships that we have to fit out, hence.' Then they were told that the best ships and the main part of the fleet were to be laid up in the Medway and flying squadrons would harass trade in the North Sea and Channel. It was a suicidal policy. The river Thames together with the river Medway made London extremely vulnerable to invasion. Queen Elizabeth had seen the necessity of a sheltered harbour where her ships could be laid up during the winter months. The River Medway, following into the Thames, was admirable for this with a good rise and fall of the tide and with a bottom of soft mud, free from rocks. Later the area round Gillingham Water and Rochester was extended and became known as Chatham Dockyard. There, in one of the grand houses by the water-front lived Peter Pett, naval commissioner and shipbuilder, descendant of the long line of shipbuilders, one of whom, Phineas Pett, had built the famous *Royal Sovereign*. Penn knew the defence of London was purely a naval task; it was not a job for a soldier, no matter how brilliant. Yet the king entrusted the defence of London to Monck and sent soldier Prince Rupert to Portsmouth with a squadron. Worst of all, the navy's best ship, the *Royal Charles,* with other first class ships were laid up like useless scrap.

Penn decided that Sheerness must now be the first line of defence. Then there must be much stronger defence for the first-class ships in the higher reaches of the Medway. To do this, a chain must be laid across the river between Gillingham and Hoo Salt Marshes, which the enemy could not break through. We have in Penn's own handwriting his 'Memorandum of his first Consultation at Sheerness' of 20th March. Those present included Commissioner Pett, shipbuilder, Phineas Pett, Captain Trafford, and many other distinguished sailors, gunners and soldiers, and fire-ships. Flag officer Sir Edward Spragg was put in command at Sheerness. There was long delay building the heavy chain which had to be supported by four wooden bridges to keep it from sinking.

On May 14th the English arrived at Breda to sign the clauses of the peace treaty. De Witt was not deterred. He set about finding pilots who knew the Medway. There were 1800 Englishmen in Dutch prisons and the Dutch offered large sums of money paid down to volunteer pilots. Many of them, press-ganged in the first place, were only too willing to oblige. On 4th June the Dutch sailed, with a large fleet, and sent a small squadron up the Thames. Then they recalled it and concentrated everything on the Medway. Still the government took no action, lulled by the arrival of a Treaty. De Witt was playing as dirty game' but a clever one. At last on 9th June Charles saw the truth and gave a panic order for fire-ships lying in the Thames.

Then on 10th June came Peter Pett's serious warning: 'The Dutch being in the Nore will get into Sheerness this evening. I doe believe the whole stresse of the business will lie at ye chain a little beyond Gillingham.' Sheerness fell because the recoil of the guns made them dig themselves into the soft sandy soil. The ordered arrival of the faulty timber was too late. This plus lack of drinking water made it impossible for the English to stay. The moment King Charles heard that Sheerness had fallen he sprang to life and ordered Monck to go to Chatham to take charge. This Monck did to the best of his incapability. He acted on impulse, owing to ignorance of an element in which he was not trained.

Pett sent soldiers from the dockyard to Upnor Castle and Gillingham and some were put on the *Charles V* and *Matthias* the guardships lying near the chain. More ships were sunk at the bend of the river. Pett wanted the *Royal Charles* to be taken higher up the reach and ordered shipwrights with their boats to tow her up. But a senior officer stopped this and sent them to sink more vessels instead on 11th June. The whole policy of Monck and others was to sink, sink, sink more and more ships and so block the river. Meanwhile Penn was living at Deptford to be there for the defence of London itself. He was not so certain as was Monck that the great ships up the Medway, such as the *Royal Charles,* were safe behind the boom and chain beyond Hoo Salt Marsh and Gillingham. He also believed the Dutch would land and set fire to Deptford Yard at dead of night. He proved to be right. The English watch were asleep at the time. Penn had the defaulters severely punished.

Penn and Pett renewed their efforts to carry *Royal Charles* higher up the river, but Monck refused he said the boom would not break. A very brave Dutchman swam beneath the cable and cut it. The Dutch following found a crew of seven on board and she was captured without opposition. De Witt had ordered his brother to humiliate the arrogant English by towing her back to Holland, where the *Royal Charles* was put on view and the Dutch flocked to see her.

While England wept and writhed at the news in humiliation, Penn's personal anguish cannot be described. The *Royal Charles* was almost himself, she was certainly the best half of his life. On her he had been sent to greet his sovereign, on her he had been knighted, on her he had won the friendship of the Duke of York, on her he had won the greatest battle fought in the Dutch wars to date. His wife and family were received as personal friends at court because of his life on board the vessel, now being gawped at by the Dutch: the ship, which, if only he and the duke had been allowed to take her out to sea, would have prevented the terrible defeat.

By now, Monck had lost his confidence. He ordered the famous ships, the *Royal Oak, Royal London* and *Royal James* to be moved and have holes cut in their sides so that they should sink. He then ordered the sinking of every ship in the river where she lay. The soldier's defence, had it not been catastrophic, would have been ludicrous and wicked. The Dutch then moved away to the estuary itself.

The king lost his popularity. Anger was rising throughout the country and parliament was called for.It was felt that lack of money did not excuse the navy having been kept in harbour. Scapegoats were sought and on the 18th Commissioner Pett, technically, though not officially, the chief officer at Chatham Dockyard, was put into the Tower.

Penn knew there would be an investigation into the defeat and that the Navy Board would take the blame despite the fact the Navy Board had acted on the orders of the king himself, obeying soldier Monck and laying up the navy instead of sending the ships out to fight. Penn went to see Sir William Batten to discuss the problem and thence to the Navy Board whence he took Pepys home to discuss how best Pepys should present their case. Pepys had already done well once before in the House of Commons and his position made him the Navy Board spokesman; the naval commanders could not act as speakers. Peter Pett was called in from the Tower and charged with not moving the great ships as instructed. As no one dared criticise Monck any more than the king himself, Pett had to be proved the culprit; and as he was no politician, Pepys found his answers very silly. The unfortunate Pett was returned to the Tower. Parliament met for a second session that year and names were hurled across the floor of the House of many men, all declared to be guilty, but the name of Penn was never once mentioned, even by his greatest enemies, Prince Rupert and the cavaliers.

Despite the havoc wrought upon England's shamefully inert navy, the Treaty of Breda was remarkably favourable to the defeated country. Both sides retained their winnings. Thus England kept New Amsterdam and its environs and called it New York. She also retained the untamed land between Hudson and the Delaware. In consequence, the entire Atlantic seaboard of North America would eventually become British. This was an historical harvest incomparably greater than the handful of eastern spice islands gained, at England's expense, by the Dutch. There were three reasons for this surprising outcome: first, the value of America was grossly underestimated by contemporaries; secondly, the Dutch were alarmed by French inroads in the Spanish Netherlands and had to concentrate their energies to meet this new potential threat. Thirdly, however, – little remarked but important – the underlying strength of the English at sea, which Penn had demonstrated at Lowestoft and nurtured at the Navy Board, made it apparent that no lasting Dutch triumph could be secured by force of arms. Political enemies had forced Penn into the penumbra of public life, where neither the credit of his victories nor the shame of England's defeats could reach him easily. Yet the part he played was well known to the king and well remembered by the duke; ten years after his death, the king gave the territory of Sylvania to Penn's son in honour of the father's services. The posthumous reward was an apposite one, for it perpetuated Penn's name in the land which his vision and perseverance had helped to win for England.

* * *

Parliament met on 10th October, generally discontented and eager for scapegoats. The king, wise to this mood, opened with a short and tactful speech: 'Some miscarriages had occasioned some differences between him and them, but now he had altered his counsels and they should henceforth agree. What had been done amiss had been done by the advice of a person now removed from his counsels.' The person was the Lord Chancellor Clarendon, father-in-law to the Duke of York. He had not been responsible for the naval debacle, but was widely blamed for the general deficiencies of royal policy.

On 15th October Penn summoned the Navy Board to meet him and prepare accounts to satisfy the commissioners of the treasury and be ready for defence questions which might be asked in parliament. A few days later parliament resolved that a committee be appointed to enquire into 'the miscarriages of the late war. It was ordered that Mr Speaker send to Sir Edward Spragg, Captain Cox and Sir William Penn to attend the House at the same time.'

This was the beginning of a campaign against him by Penn's cavalier enemies. They formed a very strong party in the House and were guided by Prince Rupert and General Monck. Rupert's enmity is understandable; Monck was jealous of Penn's fame and his friendship with the Duke of York. They both hoped the enquiry might destroy Penn and divide him from the duke. So on morning of 21st October Penn took his seat in the House for the debate of the 'miscarraige of the war and disobeying orders of H.R.H. for pursuit of victory obtained by His Highness in the first engagement against the Dutch'. As Rupert and Monck well knew, the man who was technically responsible for the slackening of the sails of the *Royal Charles* was Penn. But the evidence clearly proved the case to be quite otherwise. Grey's *Debates* give an exciting extract of the proceedings: Sir John Harman, captain of the ship, said he had no order from the duke for slackening speed by lowering sails. A cavalier M.P., Captain Cox, said he 'wondered the duke's mind should so soon be altered after giving express order to make all sail they could. But Mr Brounckner of the bedchamber who had sustained the terror on the day, resolved to prevent the like on the day succeeding.' He went to beg him to break off the engagement. He went to Penn

> He knew how miraculously the duke had been preserved that day and for the duke was heir apparent he therefore desired and advised him to order the master to slacken the sails. Penn answered him honestly He durst give no such advice, except he had a mind to be hanged, for the duke himself had given positive charge to the contrary. So Brounckner went to the master of the ship and told him it was the duke's pleasure he should slack sails. At last they put it to the question whether Brounckner should not be carried to the Tower . . . At last it ended it should be suspended till Harman came home from the West Indies.

Penn's enemies had lost their first round against him, for the final result of this enquiry was to enhance Penn's reputation. The next day Penn went into the House and sat as a member while the Medway disaster was discussed. Pepys answered all questions and they seemed fully satisfied.

Commissioner Pett of the Navy Board had been present through the proceedings. He was no politician but a magnificent craftsman and terrified of parliament. The result was he made a bad impression and was an easy scapegoat for anyone used to parliamentary proceedings.

Penn was not asked a single question. The cavalier faction knew only too well that his original advice, like that of the duke, had been totally contrary to the whole affair. Sheerness would not have fallen had the first-class ships been out beyond the Nore. The debate being now ended, the House adjourned till the next day. Pepys's mood was complacent: 'So, with our hearts very light, Sir W. Penn and I in his coach home it being now near eight o'clock.

The next day the House declared it was unnecessary to receive information from Prince Rupert and Monck concerning the miscarriages at Chatham, Sheerness and the Medway. They were given ten days to prepare their statement. Meanwhile parliament had another matter in hand and that was to rid the country of the power and presence of Clarendon. They discussed taking a vote on the impeachment of Clarendon. However the Chatham business interposed. In the words of Grey's *Debates:* 'This was the first session after the burning of the ships at Chatham by the Dutch and accordingly the Duke of Albemarle gave in'.

On studying the full text of Monck's speech, it is impossible not to be reminded of Venables reporting his failure to capture Hispaniola, to Cromwell's Council. Just as Venables had blamed everyone save only himself, for his failure, Monck did exactly the same thing. Fortunately for him, Pett in his nervousness had made a bad impression, so Monck found it easy to lay much of the blame on him. 'Pett took the boats away . . . I visited the chain . . . where I found no works for the defence of it.' Monck was lying. Pepys had recorded Penn returning from Chatham, fortifying the Medway by a chain at the stakes and ships laid there with guns. The whole of Penn's works were recorded in the Addenda to the *Calendar of Domestic Papers* of Charles II. But this was the soldier-admiral defending himself. 'All this was the fault of Commissioner Pett who had not moved the *Royal Charles* many weeks before. He ordered the famous ship to be removed at once, it was not done because Pett said he had but one pilot and the tide was on the ebb.' That the tide mattered to Penn infuriated the non-sailor Albemarle. 'I had no assistance from Commissioner Pett . . . nor no gunners, nor no men.' One notable fact about the speech should not go unremarked. Though several names were mentioned for dereliction of duty, the name of Penn never once appeared. Even the Prince and Monck did not dare accuse him. The political nation had wanted a sailor to defend the river, not a soldier, and Penn's victory in the *Royal Charles* was too fresh in Londoners' minds.

Monck escaped parliament's censure on this occasion, though even Clarendon said it was plain Monck knew not what orders to give. But as Monck made Commissioner Pett so prominent in his speech as culprit, almost organiser of the defeat, the house found Pett guilty 'of great, high crimes' and so he, walking at that time at liberty in the hall was ordered to the bar of the House and charged. He was ordered to withdraw and a committee appointed to examine 'the miscarriages of the late war which should now examine those [charges] made against Pett'.

Penn was not an active member of the House, but he did attend from time to time whenever naval matters were in question and it was possible for him to be in London. Pepys attended as a member of the public. He put in his *Diary* on 13th November, 'The House is a mighty heat against Pett, that they would have him impeached.' But it is interesting to read the debate of 14th November when a motion to speak against the order concerning commissioner Pett was made. Unfortunately we are not given the name of the member who submitted the motion: could it have been Penn? Leave was given. It was objected that 'as to Pett we have no jurisdiction of the fault to punish it'. But despite this important legal point the case dragged on for four months at the end of which he was dismissed from office, deprived of his grand house and allowed to retire to the country to end his days in peace. The reason for this last act of clemency was that it was realised in high places if the articles of impeachment were proceeded with, certain men more prominent than Pett would suffer.

The real culprits were Charles II and Monck himself: the king for his lethargy and Monck for persuading him to lay up all first-class ships and fight a defensive campaign.

Furthermore, once action started, Monck's policy had been one of self-mutilation. The English losses were shameful, chiefly because they did more damage to their own fleet than was done by the Dutch. *Royal Charles* and *Unity* captured through neglect, *Royal James, Royal Oak* and *Royal London* burned to the water's edge, *Matthew, Charles V* and *Sancta Maria,* with her valuable cargo, fired and destroyed. The English sank five fireships and three small boats at the Mussel Bank, and three good ships at the chain; this without the three men-of-war burnt at Upnor.

But the material damage did not equal the pulverising effect on English morale. The four hundred country members in the House, were many of them far more intelligent than Clarendon was prepared to believe, and they shared the exasperation of the country. One such was the member for Hull, the famous poet Andrew Marvell, perhaps the greatest lyricist England has produced, as well as being a brilliant satirist and politician. John Milton first realised his qualities and obtained him a post as Secretary under Cromwell. Born only a few days before Penn, the poet had several points in common with the admiral. Like Penn, after service under Cromwell, he was elected to the April 1660 parliament and again elected to the 1661 cavalier parliament. Also, like

Penn's son, William, he had studied at Saumur. But unlike the admiral, his pen could be biting. Satire in that era was commonly used as a political weapon. It was so used against the disgrace of the Medway. We may sample, Sir John Denham's wit first:

DIRECTIONS TO A PAINTER
Here painter, let thine art describe a story
Shaming our warlike islands ancient glory

. . .

Make the Dutch fleet, while we supinely sleep
Without opposers masters of the deep.
Draw thunder from their floating castles sent
Against our forts, weak as our Government
Draw Woolwich, Deptford, London and the Tower
Meanly abandoned to a foreign power.

Marvell brilliantly retouched this urbane caricature with his immortal poem, *The Last Instructions to a Painter.* Reading that poem of 990 lines, it is impossible not to believe that he and Penn knew each other well. Many of its lines would find an answer in the sailor's heart, such as the portion dated London, 4th September 1667:

Moncke from the bank the dismal sight does view.
Our feathered gallants, which came down that day
To be spectator of the new play
Leave him alone when first they hear the gun
                and to London run.
Our seamen, whom no danger's shape could fright,
Unpaid, refuse to mount our ships and fight.

The poem continues:
Whose counsel first did this mad war beget?
PETT, the sea-architect in making ships
Was the first cause of all these naval slips;
Had he not built, none of these faults had been.
If no Creation, there had been no Sin . . .

No finer exposition of those angry years could be made by any historian.

* * *

But the nation was more angry with Clarendon that with Pett. On 9th November when Penn was present in the House, the members first asked H.R.H. what orders he had given for the defending of Sheerness and then they went on to the impeachment of the Earl of Clarendon, as the minister ultimately responsible, for the dividing of the fleet. That same day, Penn told Pepys that Clarendon's impeachment for treason had been discussed. On 11th November a vote was taken; the voting was 161 to 89 for Clarendon to be impeached and sent to the House of Lords. However, the Lords refused to put Clarendon in prison and he fled to France on 3rd December. But the commons would not be appeased. On 18th December in the afternoon, parliament agreed to make the banishment of Clarendon permanent, sixty-five votes to forty-two.

CHAPTER NINE

The Shadow of Disgrace

Although Penn's talent for command had been frustrated by the machinations of his enemies, two sources of consolation remained to him. His reputation for probity was unassailed; and his family was united and loving. Now, however, in the last triennium of his life, the shadows which had been cast across his career moved to threaten his most intimate and important funds of happiness.

The autumn had been clouded by Sir William Batten's death on 5th October; he had been such an old friend, his career so closely connected, his progress *pari passu,* with Penn's own, that the loss was deeply affecting. Penn found it hard to recover his accustomed merriment after this blow. His wife dispelled the gloom by frequent excursions to the theatre. The Penns now had a country house of sorts which they rented at Walthamstow, where they entertained the Pepys, and the Navy Board parties went regularly to town to see Shakespeare's comedies performed. When parliament rose on 9th December, 1667, – 'Christmas drawing near,' the royal writ declared, 'His Majesty conceives it seasonable to return to your homes' – it may have seemed that there was a chance of a peaceful, even a happy Christmas for the Penns. The Duke of York's recovery from a dangerous bout of smallpox saved a friend and patron whom Penn both loved and needed. And the news that young Margaret was about to give him a grandchild and would be at home for the birth inspired Penn with the hope that he would be able to draw his beloved family around him for a joyful event.

The fragile hope was first threatened and dashed by the conduct of his son, William. The boy's behaviour during his absence in Ireland had been wayward and equivocal. He still affected the dress and manners of a courtier: George Fox, asked by the anxious boy whether he should cease to sport a sword, advised him, 'Wear it as long as thou canst.' It would be long before young Penn abandoned it. Meanwhile, however, his Quaker associations had grown more numerous and profound. At one moment, he was seized at a Quaker meeting by over-zealous constabulary and flung into gaol. The embarrassed prison governor released him as soon as he was recognised and sent him to Broghill; Broghill wrote to Penn and Penn to William, but the boy seemed incorrigible. His father ordered him peremptorily home.

A rupture was inevitable. William was intractable to rational argument, partly because he was genuinely possessed by the fervour of a neophyte, partly becase he was suffering from a syndrome of indigenous depression, which stimulated his conversion by giving him enhanced spiritual awareness, while also making him moody and unpredictable. Penn, on the other hand, was not yet willing to make compromises with Quakerism. As we have seen, the family cultivated tolerance and respected dissent; Penn's wife had, evidently, a genuine regard for Quaker piety. Membership of the sect, however, was quite another matter. It brought social stigma and civil disabilities; Penn hated to see his son bring these things on himself. It has long been thought that the admiral was also concerned about the implications for his own position: the story – merely an unverifiable anecdote – that he sought, and even was offered, the earldom of Weymouth; that he intended to build up a lavish patrimony and found an aristocratic dynasty; that he aimed to set himself up in a country mansion for the purpose: all this gossip has fed the supposition that Penn's break with his son was caused by William's self-disqualification from the peerage and Quaker contempt for wordly honours. The theory is unacceptable. The only evidence for any part of it is Pepys avowal that Penn expressed an interest in Sir Robert Brooke's 'fine house at Wanstead'. Yet the terms in which Pepys continues makes it clear that this cannot have been part of a plan of aristocratic arrogation on Penn's part. 'He did intende to pull down that house and build a less and that he should get £1500 by the old house and I know not what foolness. I never will believe he intended to buy it.'

Rather, the rift between the generations is sufficiently explained by the general suspicion or odium in which Quakerism was held. The Quakers' calculated disruptions of church services were thought dangerous to the state. Their pacifism was potentially treasonable. In the plague year, two thousand of them were imprisoned and others deported to Jamaica: their role was that of traditional outcasts and social scapegoats. Even if their heresies could be tolerated, their embarrassing and disreputable antics were impossible to bear in individual cases, especially those of otherwise respectable men. Penn, for instance, was shocked, on the day before the signing of the Treaty of Breda, to see the fashionable music-master, Solomon Eccles, walk naked through Westminster Hall, with a chafing dish full of fire and brimstone on his head, crying out, 'Repent! Repent!' Young William never indulged in such excesses but Quaker circles can hardly have seemed, to his father, a suitable milieu.

The rift came in three stages. First, William publicly challenged his father on his arrival home by addressing him as 'thou'. This pronoun was not used in polite society, except to address menials and in prayer or worship. Its adoption by Quakers implied mutual humiliation, at one level, and at another, the mutual divine recognition which inspired all their common dealings – the awareness of the indwelling spirit of God in every man. William must have used it without intending disrespect: indeed, he addressed the king by it without causing offence. Yet his father seems to have seen it as a symbol of William's continuing adherence to Quakerism and – what was perhaps just as bad – of filial disobedience.

William's second and third offences strained his relations with his father to breaking point. He refused to take part in the family Christmas festivities which had been anticipated with so much warmth; and, worse still, when young Peg was delivered of a bonny daughter, named Margaret after her mother and grandmother, he declined to attend the christening. The interview to which the admiral summoned his son in his carriage next day was acerbic. In the ensuing months, though mutual affections never died, they grew ever further apart, and William, who had promised to be a cause of pride to his parents, became an additional source of anguish and strain in what was anyway to be a time of agony.

For, in the spring of 1668, Penn was confronted by a final, and almost fatal re-mobilisation of the forces of his political enemies. Rupert and Monck had probably prepared their strategy for Penn's undoing in the dying days of the previous parliament. On 3rd December, 1667, Penn had been summoned to the committee enquiring into naval misconduct and asked for an account of the notorious incident in which Sandwich had pillaged the two India Prize Ships of 1665. Penn had attended enough committees to know how they could turn innocent remarks to their victims' destruction. He stated merely that Sandwich had acted in accordance with the advice of the chief officers and that it was what admirals before had done. Penn's personal conduct was not called in question. Indeed, as we have seen, he had not connived in the affair; rather, he had actually opposed it in writing. Yet his position was not unassailable. Like other officers, he had received a share of the booty and it was not easy to show that his profits had excluded goods seized illicitly from beneath the broken bulkheads. Though he could retire from the committee with an easy conscience, he may have felt a twinge of apprehension of what further enquiries might lie ahead. The next campaign against Penn was in the making. Only an opportunity was wanting, and was about to be supplied.

In the Spring of 1668, the king and Duke and York were surfeited of land-admirals and decided to appoint Sir William Penn to command the fleet for the summer's expedition. Penn felt his former health and vigour to have ebbed and he beseeched his Majesty to withdraw his gracious intention. But the king and duke insisted he became commander. Now, therefore, the chief pre-occupation of Prince Rupert and Monck was to prevent Penn's going to sea. No one could countermand the Lord High Admiral: was there any other way of obtaining the result they so keenly wanted?

While M.P.s were making their preliminary enquiries, Penn went to his home in Walthamstowe to see the sorrowing widow and family of his old friend Sir William Batten. They had been left badly off. Penn tried to arrange some money due from the Navy Board and so failed to attend parliament for several days. Thus he missed as Pepys said 'the several motions made for calling strictly again upon the miscarriages; particularly in the business of the prizes and the not prosecuting the first victory, only to give affront to Sir W. Penn, whose going to sea this year doth give them matter of great dislike'. Pepys continued, 'I am sorry that he should have this fall so unhappily, without any fault, but rather merit of his own that made him fitter for command than anybody else.' This is the most astonishing statement in the whole of Pepys' *Diary*. From first to last it is Penn whom he hates and denigrates, yet he was compelled to acknowledge the truth which caused his jealousy: Penn, whom he stigmatised as a 'common tarpaulin', was England's greatest sailor.

It was on 30th March that the duke declared he would go to sea with the summer expedition. It was indeed, an act 'of mighty hot friendship' on the duke's part. Monck and Rupert went into immediate consultation and they found a way to stop Penn sailing: by the only possible legal way. That way was by impeachment. No one under impeachment could leave the shores of England until he was cleared of the charges brought against him. This had to be debated and voted upon in parliament. Then the written charges were sent to the House of Lords, where a similar procedure was followed. The Lords then sent their answer back to the Commons who did, or did not, vote an impeachment. It all took time, but it also took time to find grounds on which to impeach the admiral and general at sea.

They had failed recently in the slackening of sail and in the Medway disaster. They cast their minds further back. There was the scandal of the Earl of Sandwich who had broken bulk in 1665. Penn had gone to sea as vice-admiral to Sandwich. It would be easy enough to find witnesses against Penn among cavalier M.P.s The chief technical difficulty – the limitations of parliamentary jurisdiction – could safely be ignored by the conspirators. Monck knew that illegal breaking of bulk came under the power of the commissioners of accounts, from which there was no appeal, for the court was not responsible to parliament. If it had not been the all-powerful Monck and Rupert who pressed for Penn's impeachment, the commissioners would have stood out against this attack on their prerogative.

On Monday, the 13th April, Samuel Pepys 'went to the commissioners of treasury and so to Westminster by water, with G. Montagu and others and spoke all in trouble about the prize business'. That same afternoon the House of Commons ordered Penn to attend the next morning.

For Penn, this summons to the House was a shot through the heart. Why should the House of Commons wish him to attend when it had been made clear that the Lord High Admiral, the Duke of York himself, was going to sea this season? For that meant he would be going too. Of course he knew trouble was brewing, but how could it affect his order to sail with the Lord High Admiral?

Fortunately it is possible to follow the whole of the proceedings in the House of Commons on that terrible Tuesday, the 14th, because they were noted down, in abridgement by Anchitell Grey, M.P. for Derby, in the diary which he kept of *Debates* which interested him most. Although he could not write down speeches verbatim and many were omitted altogether, Grey's *Debates* generally gives a far fuller account of what was actually said than does the Official Journal of the House of Commons. The following account of what Penn had to endure on 14th is taken from Grey.

A narrative was brought into the House by Sir Thomas Lee from the commissioners of accounts; and the matter relating to Sir William Penn, as to the embezzling of prize-goods was debated. SIR WILLIAM PENN denies all charges of embezzling goods. This being the first time he has heard the charge, desires a few days time to give such answer as he will abide by.

Sir ROBERT ATKINS, K.B. [Afterwards Lord Chief Justice of the Common Pleas]: The commissioners of accounts have power to hear and determine. What encouragement will these gentlemen have if we give an appeal from them? Therefore would know whether it be a charge, or a conviction.

SIR WILLIAM PENN: Many possibly who have been punished for some misdemeanours, may have given this information therefore desires he may have time to give in his answer, which he hopes will be to the satisfaction of the house.

MR. COVENTRY [brother of Sir William Coventry]: No man's single aye or no, does condemn or acquit. Hopes that no subject, much less a member of this house, shall be censured without hearing. He was never summoned before the commissioners of accounts.

MR VAUGHAN: Captain Jeffreys, without any order, did break bulk. Some of the flag-officers took more than the proportion allotted. That Penn took more than the proportion allotted to him is his charge. If he were not a member, you could not hear him, because of the power of the commissioners of accounts; he, not being before them, may be heard by you.

The accurate legal implications of this speech would give many cause to wonder why the affair was made the subject of an impeachment and not a trial by the commissioners of accounts. Finally Sir William Penn rose.

SIR WILLIAM PENN: I went on board, with Sir William Berkeley by command of Lord Sandwich; but only to keep persons from ill-purposes. I did sell some goods, but know not how much. And I say farther, that no goods were sold, till Lord Sandwich gave them the king's warrant.

MR SEYMOUR, speaker: The method of proceedings in this house is, for a member in his place, to answer to his charge and then withdraw.

After Sir William Penn had withdrawn he was allowed till Thursday to prepare his answer. He was fully aware that he was the victim of a political manoeuvre organised to keep him on shore until the fleet had sailed. The next morning, as he walked through Whitehall, he passed the king and called out to him, 'Sir, I am your martyr?' When he drove to the House on Thursday, 16th April, 1668, he knew he was facing a harder battle than his battles at sea. It was a new experience and one for which he had no training. His great source of comfort was the Duke of York, who made it clear that, as Penn could not go to sea while under impeachment charges, he, the Lord High Admiral, would not go to sea either. His anger at this treatment of the sailor whom he had chosen to command the summer expedition went very deep, for the friendship between these two men is one of the remarkable friendships in history. So, as Penn was walking to his seat in the Commons, the duke was nearby in Whitehall waiting anxiously to hear the result of the debate. Grey wrote the proceedings in his journal.

SIR WILLIAM PENN'S ANSWER, IN HIS PLACE, TO THE CHARGE OF EMBEZZLING PRIZE-GOODS: Sir William Berkeley commanded him on board, where he was not above a quarter of an hour, and did not break bulk. The captain that informs was twelve months in the Indies; and he wonders how he could give evidence to the commissioners of accounts. He denies not the sale of goods to the value of 850 shillings; the other goods he sold but they were Sir William Berkeley's. (He withdrew of his own acord).

MR WELD informs the house, that one Gory informed him, that Sir William Penn was the first man that gave advice to Lord Sandwich to break bulk.

MR COVENTRY thinks us not ripe to give any judgement in the business. The order came from Lord Sandwich and until he comes home you can neither acquit nor condemn; things must be done *juste*, as well as *justum*.

SIR ROBERT ATKINS: Sir William Penn has this which falls out luckily for him. The Earl of Sandwich is absent and Sir William Berkeley dead. You cannot expect so much proof as to convict him, but there is certainly grounds sufficient to impeach him.

Other members spoke after hearing this strange attitude towards justice. Then

SIR WILLIAM COVENTRY hopes you will not impeach any member without propable grounds at least to condemn him. It appears not that Sir William Penn converted one halfpenny-worth of goods to his own use, which were not granted by the privy-seal afterwards.

Penn was then suspended from sitting. A committee was appointed to draw up an impeachment against him and to search into precedents in relation to the suspension of members from sitting whilst they were under impeachment. The question then being propounded that an impeachment be made against Sir Wm Penn . . . was resolved in the affirmative and ordered that it be referred to a committee of twenty-four. Of the twenty-four named not one would appear to be a friend of Penn.

Penn made no attempt to hide himself from public view. Pepys says Penn turned up at the office on Saturday morning, 'seemingly merry' and on Sunday went to church as usual. No mean feat, for in those days impeachment could end in death.

When the case went to the Lords, the duke himself took the chair, with the result that the account of the proceedings is laid out in the House of Lords *Journal* in a manner very distinctive from their usual recordings of their debates. The House gave order, that Sir William Penn should be brought to the bar, which was accordingly done, by the Gentleman Usher of the Black Rod; he kneeling until the Lord Keeper bade him stand up. And then his Lordship told him, 'He was impeached, by the Commons of England assembled in parliament, in the name of themselves and of all the Commons of England, for several high crimes and misdemeanours committed by him; which charge should be read unto him.'

As he stood there facing the duke, Penn knew he had one friend in that powerful House, but how many more would only later be revealed. The real ordeal was just beginning. The articles against him were read, and comprised

1. First, in or about the month of September, 1665, the *Golden Phoenix* and the *Slothany,* two ships belonging to the United Provinces of the Netherlands, were taken at sea, as prize, during the late war, by his Majesty's fleet then under the command of the Earl of Sandwich in which said fleet Sir William Penn was the vice-admiral and commander-in-chief under the said earl. The said Sir William

Penn, did, contrary to his allegiance, duty, commission and articles of war established by this present parliament . . . for his singular lucre . . . conspire and advise with several persons, to open the holds of the said ships, divers and sundry times, before judgement thereof first passed the Admiralty court, and took out and embezzled great quantities of rich goods, whereby his Majesty was defrauded of one hundred and fifteen thousand pounds, besides rich jewels.

2.   Secondly, the said Sir William Penn in pursuit of the said conspiracy, did, on or about the 14th September, repair on board the said *Slothany,* in the company of Sir William Berkeley, vice-admiral to the white squadron commanded by the said Sir William Penn, and gave order to the captain of the *Slothany* to follow directions given by Sir William Berkeley, who immediately caused the hatchways of the ship to be broke open, and took out bales of silk, mace and other goods to great value and carried them away . . . and afterwards this action was repeated several times and great quantities of rich goods carried away.

3.   Thirdly, he, the said Sir William Penn converted a considerable portion of the goods to his own use and did sell divers parcels of the said goods.

4.   Fourthly, the better to colour fraud and embezzlement, orders were obtained from the said Earl of Sandwich, bearing dates of 15th and 21st September, 1665, for the taking and distributing some part of the said goods among several officers of whom Sir William Penn was one, and had a great proportion allotted to him, although he knew very well that the said orders of the Earl of Sandwich were void, and contrary to the commission of the said Earl and the law of the land. Afterwards, a warrant, dated 17th October, 1665, was unduly procured from his Majesty for distributing the said goods . . . and the said Commons to pray that the said Sir William Penn . . . receive such condign punishment, as the same shall deserve and that further proceedings may be, upon every one of them, had and used against him as is agreeable to law and justice.

When the articles had been read to him, the Lord Keeper asked him 'What said he to them? He replied that he looked upon himself as a very unhappy man to be brought hither upon this account; but it was his comfort, that he should have such honourable judges. He desired a short day might be given him, to put his answer in writing; and that counsel might be assigned to him'. After this he withdrew and the House 'directed that he should have a copy of his charges, and that he should put his answer in writing on Wednesday morning next. So he was called in again, and told their decision and asked what counsel he desired to have? He named six councillors and this the House ordered accordingly.'

During Penn's appearance in the Lords, the duke said nothing, but his presence ensured, as Pepys tells us, that his friend 'was used mighty civilly'. More than that, to see him in the chair must have been pure spiritual comfort to Penn, for the duke by no means made a point of regular attendance at the House of Lords as is proved by their Journal. He was there because Penn was there and Penn was in trouble. The duke knew that the cause of the trouble was a tissue of lies brought forward by jealous enemies. He was again in the chair on the following Wednesday, the day the House had ordered Penn to appear and put in his answer. The House of Lords *Journal* shows a great number of lords attended than was usual.

This day Sir William Penn, according to the order of this House on the 27th instant, being appointed to put in his answer to the impeachment of the House of Commons against him, was brought to the bar by the Gentleman Usher; and having kneeled until the Lord Keeper commanded him to stand up, he humbly presented his said answer; which was read as follows.

1. To the first article, doth say that he, this defendant is not guilty of any crime objected against him in the first article. He did not break bulk.

2. To the second article he saith; that on or about 14th of September, he did go on board the said *Slothany,* in the company of the said Sir William Berkeley, being required so to do by the said Earl of Sandwich, but doth deny that he did then, or at any other time go on board the *Slothany* in pursuance of the said conspiracy in the first said article; or that he did command the captain to give way or permit Sir W. Berkeley to take away any of the said goods; or that he sent any men on board the *Slothany* to assist Sir William Berkeley in breaking open the hatchways of the said ship and carrying away bales of silk, mace or goods whatsoever.

3. To the Third Article this defendant doth answer, that true it is that nineteen bales of silk and one half of silk, ten bales of cinnamon,

two bags of nutmegs, eight bags of pepper and one punch of cloves, were taken out of the *Slothany* and *Phoenix,* by way of distribution among the flag-officers, and did come into the hands of this defendant, as his share, and were sold and converted by him to his own use, by virtue of the said order of the Earl of Sandwich, bearing the date of the 15th and 21st September 1665 and by virtue of his Majesty's warrant dated October 17th 1665. But this defendant denies that he had or sold to his own use, any other goods than those above mentioned.

4.   To the Fourth article . . . The said order of the Earl of Sandwich were not obtained by him, the defendant, and he denies that his Majesty's warrant . . . was by him or by any other person by his direction, procured from his Majesty . . . further he denies he did take the said four bales, or eight suckles out of the said *Phoenix* or *Slothany,* or that he did sell or dispose of the same to his own use or advantage . . . All which matters he this defendant is ready to prove.

The Lord's *Journal* records the curious conclusion of their enquiry, by which Penn was effectively vindicated: 'A message was sent to the House of Commons, by John Cool and Sir Walter Littleton; to let them know, that Sir William Penn hath this day put in his answer in writing to their Impeachment against him; a copy whereof the Lords have sent to the House of Commons.'

But the Lords made no indictment whatsoever against Penn. Instead they returned his answer, which affirmed his innocence, as their own answer. Therefore, their declaration and judgement was that Sir William Penn was innocent. The letter was laid on the Secretary's table, in the Commons, on the same day. Pepys noted, the House of Commons 'did not read it nor take notice of it, so as I believe they will by design defer it till they rise, that so, he, by lying under an impeachment, may be prevented in his going to sea; which will vex him and trouble the Duke of York'. It did indeed vex Penn, who told Pepys that he was labouring to have his answer, but believed he would, by design, be prevented from going to sea that year. Pepys, however, was misinformed for, according to the Commons *Journal,* 'on May 4th, five days after receiving the letter, the Commons did read Penn's answer and referred it to the committee which had drawn up the articles of impeachment. They were to consider it and send up a replication to the Lords'. Doubtless the duke got wind of the intended replication, for it was no mere coincidence that on the very same day the *Journal* of the House of Lords reads: 'On 4th May it was ordered no Lords go out of town so as to be absent from the House during the sitting of the House.' They dealt with numerous bills from the commons. But they did not deal with the replication, for the Commons never sent it; it lay till they adjourned on 9th May. As the Commons had sent no answer to the Lords' judgement of 'not guilty' to the impeachment, Penn was never legally impeached.

The matter was never again mentioned in either House. The proceedings had fulfilled their purpose, for the fleet had sailed for the summer season, leaving Penn on shore, to the delight of Monck and Rupert, who now commanded the fleet together. As Penn had not sailed, the duke did not sail either. He stayed on shore to support his admiral. The duke's behaviour was a regal act of friendship. The cavalier parliament made no attempt to have Penn removed from his position of one of the principal officers and commissioners of the navy; outfaced by an innocent man and a constant friend, the campaign against Penn subsided.

The great artists of the day paint the Duke of York as a handsome man with a long, aristocratic nose. But they key to his character lay in those blue eyes, thoughtful, serene, penetrating. The eyes of an intelligent man who could be shrewd in the extreme and hide all feeling, as surely they must have done while he sat in the chair in the lords, as remote as the Speaker in the House of Commons.

Perhaps it should be noted here that Sir William Penn for many years received no pay; the accumulated arrears of which, added to the moneys advanced by him at various times for the service of his country (one must remember the Bristol Merchant Venturers from whence some of his private fortune must have come) left his estate, at the time of his death, a creditor to the crown up upwards of £12,000. This debt was never discharged in money, but was virtually liquidated twelve years later by the gift of the province of Pennsylvania, granted to his son, William, in memory of the admiral's services to his country.

* * *

After the most dramatic and disturbing month of his whole life, Penn was suddenly faced with similar troubles affecting his great friend, the Duke of Ormonde, the Lord Lieutenant of Ireland, who arrived unexpectedly in London on 6th May, just before parliament went into recess, to defend himself against a possible impeachment. In his case also the motive was jealousy. Ormonde had been the king's most loyal friend from the beginning and this was galling to the royal favourite, the Duke of Buckingham, and his faction, who were beginning to oust all the king's former advisers. Buckingham had been the king's companion from boyhood days because his father had once been Charles I's closest friend. Another man who had recently become eager for Ormonde's impeachment, was Orrery, lord president of Munster, formerly Lord Broghill, whom Penn had formerly taken to Kinsale in the *Fellowship*. This quarrel between two old friends was a true grief to him.

During the whole of May Penn had periodical attacks of gout. On the 27th Pepys went to see him to verify that he was out of action; when Lord Brounckner fell ill also, Pepys began to feel confident of his own indispensability. But a fortnight later Penn was present at the vital committee meeting with the Duke of York and the lords of the treasury concerning the cost of the fleet. Buckingham was beginning to show his hand. He strongly objected to money spent on ships and men which could be better used for his pleasure. He wanted to stop the issue of tickets in lieu of salaries; the effect would be to conserve the king's resources, but also to leave seamen without the means of life. Buckingham was not concerned with the sufferings of men who had served their country for years. But Penn was. With Brounckner, Middleton and Pepys, he drew up a paper to prove the impossibility, without dishonour, of dispensing with tickets unless cash were provided in its place. After a heated discussion in the presence of the king, they presented the paper drawn up at the Navy Office on 10th July:

> May it please your Lordships . . . every seaman discharged, hath a right of demanding and receiving his wages, at the instant of his discharge. But, as this cannot be expected at all times in each ship without a stock of money to satisfy on board the wages of each man discharged . . . the person is become content to receive a certificate from the officers of the ship . . . which signed by us, becomes a ticket authorising the treasurer of the navy to pay him on shore . . . but as we conceive your Lordships' intention to be to put a stop to the whole use of tickets; our humble answer is every seaman discharged

hath a right of receiving his own on board, or a ticket to demand it on shore.

Buckingham's suggestion was more than curious, that the Navy Board could be relieved of its debts by not paying them! The privy council had to drop the disgraceful, cruel suggestion. The following November Buckingham had his revenge. It was when Penn, worn out by ill health was trying hard to resign as controller of the navy and take on the easier post of victualler to the navy as watchdog to the spending of naval money. At the council meeting, Buckingham led the outcry, 'It was a strange thing to thrust office into the hands of one who stands accused in parliament!' The Duke of York's attempt to make Penn a member of the privy council, was frustrated by Buckingham's influence over the king. But the duke got Penn named as a victualling contractor. So Penn went daily to Whitehall to the duke as usual and dined there merrily as before. He went a second time to St Bartholomew's Fair to see the dancing mare, and this time the poor mare forgot some of her steps to the vast entertainment of the man who had just been dealing so seriously with is seamen's tickets.

The next blow to befall Penn was more ominous, as it menaced the ducal patronage on which he depended for so much. Pepys was deeply interested in Penn's ill-health. He hoped to replace him at the Navy Board and wrote a speech for the duke to read to the board, as though written by the duke himself, decrying absences from board meetings and naming Penn in particular. It seemed to Penn that his one great friend had turned against him. He therefore wrote a long apology to his patron.

> May it please your Royal Highness, In obedience to your Royal Highness' commands directed to the Board, requiring our several answers to the matter therein expressed, as they touch our particular and general duties, I humbly take leave to offer . . . I am not conscious of at any time been wanting, by advising or assisting any member thereof; if any particular be instanced I shall not doubt of giving your Royal Highness full satisfaction therein.

Then followed many details of service with proof of his constant attendance at meetings unless employed in the service of the navy elsewhere. He mentions that the previous summer, for the recovery of his health, he hired a dwelling distant six miles from London where he went on Saturday nights, but from the first alarm of the Dutch fleet's coming to the buoy of the Nore, until the time of their departure he was the whole time at Gravesend, Woolwich, Deptford, or upon the river. He recalled 1664 when the duke sent him to Portsmouth two times. Then when H.R.H. decided to hazard his own person in time of war, Penn was sent to command the fitting of the great ships. Then very early in Spring 1665, 'Your Royal Highness was pleased to command me on board the *Royal Charles* in the Downs . . . my continuance on board the *Royal Charles* was till Christmas '65.'

The duke did everything possible to soothe his friend's feelings. Publicly he made it plain that he held Penn in as high regard as ever for he 'authorised, empowered and required Sir William Penn, Knt, to forthwith call and assemble a court-martial consisting of captains and commanders . . . to enquire concerning the loss of his Majesty's ship *Defiance* lately burned in the river near Chatham.'

* * *

The duke's action said more than any words could have done. Nor could it have come at a more fortunate time, for Penn's rupture with his son had become apparently irremediable. Although William Penn had now recovered from his extreme religious mania, under the influence of George Fox he went about preaching. In the home counties his meeting was broken up by a magistrate who recognised the son of the admiral. So, instead of imprisoning him, he wrote to Penn saying his son 'had been making a tumult'. Sir William called his son home in a fury and this time William was confronted by both parents. At this terrible interview his beloved father 'bid him take his clothes and begone from his house.'

William left home and continued preaching. Many people who would never have gone to hear Quakers, flocked to hear the famous admiral's son preach, frequently using metaphors relating to the sea. Suddenly William Penn became immensely popular, to the horror of the stalwarts of the established church who complained to the Bishop of London.

The censorship of the press was in the hands of the church and no book could be printed without a licence from the Bishop of London. William had put himself in the wrong by neglecting to obtain such a licence for his anti-trinitarian pamphlet, *The Sandy Foundation Shaken*. The printer, John Derby, was put in the Gatehouse Prison. The moment the admiral's son heard of the arrest he came forward and surrendered himself to Lord Arlington, the Secretary of State, whom he knew very well. He was put in the Tower of London and kept there from 12th December until 28th July following. Within an hour of the Tower Gates closing on William, Arlington rode in and questioned him and was perfectly satisfied William was no delinquent. So he left, promising to use his utmost to get him out.

The governor of the Tower, Sir John Robinson, was an old friend of the admiral and a frequent visitor to the Penn's house. But his friendship with William's father did not allow of any relaxation of discipline for his prisoner, who was denied the usual liberties of a political prisoner, such as exercise or walks on parole. The admiral made no attempt to communicate with him for the first few months, though he was informed of his son's condition through his personal servant who was allowed the very unusual favour of visiting his young master daily, in the presence of the Keeper. The admiral waited eagerly for a sign of submission, but the only message he got was 'Thou mayst tell my father, 'my prison shall be my grave before I will budge one jot.' This message really marked the beginning of reconciliation between them, and in later years the understanding between them was entire.

The Tower had always been a familiar object to the Penn family, both from without and within. They had always lived near it. The admiral had been imprisoned there three times. William was following his father's footsteps, save that he occupied himself by writing a book. This was a tour-de-force of memory, for he was allowed no reference books. Entitled *No Cross, No Crown,* it was a history of the intolerances and vices of familiar society. When the admiral heard of the book, he remakred with a flash of his old wit that it was a serious *cross* to him! But he must have admired the son to whom honours might come with ease, but who preferred to write that 'the alluring honours of this world were the portion of a fool and to lead a spiritual life instead.' The book passed into a hundred editions after both father and son were dead and is still read today.

While William was in the Tower, the king sent his chaplain, Dr Edward Stillingfleete, 'to conferre with him in order to the convincing of his heretical opinions'. This was on 4th January 1669. The two young men became life-long friends, but the young chaplain based his arguments on the king's favour and preferments. This was fatal. William refused to recant and remained in the Tower.

One very strange fact about the year 1668 now closing, was that Pepys, hating Penn as he did, never once mentions anywhere in his *Diary* that young William Penn was imprisoned in the Tower, though he had gleefully told the reported tale of the admiral's imprisonment there 'in a dungeon . . . where he cried like a common seaman'. Was it that, having no son of his own, he admired the young man but could not bear to say so?

CHAPTER TEN

Defiance *and Death*

The Spring of 1669 was not a happy one for the Penns nor for their closest friends. The admiral's increasing ill-health compelled him to resign from the Navy Board. He gave up his house in Navy Gardens to his successor, Viscount Brounckner, who brought his mistress to live in the rooms where Anthony Lowther had courted Peg Penn. The Penns now lived wholly in the country, at Wanstead, though not necessarily in Sir Robert Brooke's old house, an hour's ride from Whitehall. And they were lonely. Peg had begun her own family in Yorkshire; Richard was in Italy with a tutor for his health; William was in the Tower. In different circumstances it could have been a honeymoon long desired, but her husband's constant pain and a mother's concern over her two sons, damped Margaret's Irish gaiety. Admiral Batten was buried in the churchyard.

Finally there came distressing news of friends. Although Ormonde had not been impeached, as his enemies had hoped, he had been finally dismissed from his office of Lord Lieutenant of Ireland. England staggered at Ormonde's fall. He had been regarded as the king's greatest, richest and most loyal subject 'with more acres of land than anyone else and done more for the king than anyone else'. Penn did not live to see his friend returned to his original office. Meanwhile his whole world seemed crumbling round him. It may have been the duke's concern over Penn's health which held back the enquiry he was to head concerning the loss of the *Defiance,* for the actual warrant was not issued until 10th March. Hence Pepys's delight at receiving the Duke of York's commission to the Captain of the *Jerzy,* 'which do give me occasion of much mirth'.

But there was little mirth for Penn that day. Another long-time friend, Sir William Coventry, had the week before joined his son William in the Tower. Though Coventry shared the imprisonment he did not share the hardships. He was a political prisoner of

Buckingham's, which gentleman, still pursuing his ambition to fill all the offices of the crown with his own friends, had failed to dislodge the capable Coventry from the treasury and the king's favour. So he decided to hold him up to ridicule on the stage, but the plan leaked out and Coventry challenged Buckingham to a duel. Duelling was the one social custom which Charles II hated with the utmost sterness and refused to allow. Coventry found himself in the Tower.

He was given a lodging in the Brick Tower, beside the armoury and there he received as many as sixty coaches a day. All his friends called on him, to the vast annoyance of the king, who released him after two weeks. Nevertheless, Buckingham had won, for Coventry was by now so sickened of court intrigue that he retired from his post as treasurer and never again accepted public office. 'So,' wrote Pepys, 'Sir W. Coventry being gone, the king will have no good counsellor left, nor the Duke of York any friend to stick to him.' But Penn remained a victualler at the Navy Board on the insistence of the duke, who badly needed a sailor's counsel.

The *Defiance* inquiry was resumed on 1st April, Penn being slightly better. It was held on a yacht on the river. But by 25th April it had been transferred to the *Charles* and Pepys wrote, 'I did manage the business, and lay the law open to them . . . and had given my thoughts', which were to the effect that the gunner responsible for the incendiary discharge deserved death. Then Pepys had to withdraw, 'not being of the Court' for here the death sentence was concerned only genuine naval officers under the naval Deputy Judge Advocate, as the duke had stipulated to Penn, could guide the officers in matters of such importance. Their judgement was that the gunner should stand on the quarter-deck, with his fault written on his breast and a halter round his neck and so made incapable of service. Fortunately for the culprit, Pepys formed a minority of one. As Pepys's *Diary* ends on 31st May, we are left with that bitter taste of a viciously, vastly entertaining man.

For months Penn had begged the duke to let him resign from the Navy Board, but the duke would not let him go until he had found another naval man in his place. Within a month of the end of the inquiry, the king consented to let Sir Jeremy Smith take over Penn's duties. This was excellent news, for he was a good sailor, chosen by the duke. Penn stayed on as one of the Victuallers, and continued to attract many tokens of devotion from the service, and letters from shipboard correspondents acquainting him with affairs at sea. This was impressive evidence of the esteem and confidence of his fellow-sailors.

* * *

Penn's last year was at hand. The confidence of old comrades-in-arms consoled him. The restoration of amity with his son reconciled him to death. In May, 1669, the admiral at last choked back his pride and approached the duke to petition on William's behalf, to procure his release from the Tower or, at least, some mitigation of his circumstances. Speedy bringing-to-trial would be a merciful release. The duke acted with his customary loyalty and humanity. It came to light that the Bishop of London, who had committed young Penn, had never examined the book in the case; nor could he demonstrate any blasphemy or actionable heresy in it. William's fellow-sufferer, meanwhile, had been released unconditionally on the plea of his wife. His continued imprisonment was a nonsense which a word from the throne would dispel. On 28th July, the word was spoken. The king ordered William Penn's release and restoration to the bosom of his family.

As the differences of principle between father and son remained unresolved, it was wise to keep some distance between them. Only two years before, Penn had written to Ormonde to say that he hoped to settle in Ireland: that plan was now impossible, with Ormonde disgraced and Penn enfeebled, but the estates remained to care for and William's despatch to look after them seemed a serviceable solution to more than one problem.

By the spring of 1670, however, Penn felt death stirring at his side – closer than he had felt it before, unless at the height of a battle. But in the old days, when he faced death in arms, he had the strength to overcome. Now strength was draining away. He needed his son. 'I wish you had well done your business there,' he wrote in his letter of summons, 'for I find myself to decline.' William hurried to England. He had become Ireland's most prominent Quaker and was always courteously treated on his own side of the water. English society, however, was less tolerant. The Conventicle Act, which prohibited dissenters' meetings, under severe penalties, short of death, was now renewed; for the church was feeling insecure, with the Duke of York an avowed Roman Catholic and the King secretly pledging, in the Treaty of Dover, to restore the Roman Catholic faith amongst his subjects. None of this deterred William from preaching, but all went without incident until Sunday, 14th June, when William went to the Gracechurch Street Meeting House and began to speak. When he ended, he was arrested with his friend, Captain William Meade, interrogated by the Lord Mayor and committed to Newgate 'for a riot'. There was no talk of the Tower this time; Newgate was the prison for common criminals. The next day he wrote to his distracted father, 'He told me I should have my hat pulled off, for all I was Admiral Penn's son . . . that starved the seamen . . . Now dear father, be not grieved or displeased, I doubt not but I may be at liberty in a day or two to see thee . . . Thy ever obedient son.'

William had been thoroughly trained in law at the admiral's insistence – not for such an event, but to enable him to take high office. He turned the legal battle into a naval one. His first questions were those of reconnaissance, requiring to know upon what law he was prosecuted, for he had broken no law. 'The Common Law', replied the Recorder, already stung by the defendant's tactics. William demanded that the Common Law be produced. Angered at this, the Recorder replied, 'The question is whether you are guilty of this indictment.' Then William led his argument, like one of his father's lines of battle, straight into the central position of his opponent: 'The question is not whether I am guilty of this indictment, but whether this indictment be legal.' The jury gave a verdict of 'Guilty of speaking in Gracechurch Street', equivalent to an acquittal: 'speaking' was no crime, even under the Conventicle Act. They were shut up for the night and the next morning returned the same verdict. To the fury of the judge, the jury had won. Today a commemorative tablet on the wall of the Old Bailey shows where one of the most important trials in English history took place, for it established the right of trial by jury and ended the custom of the judge being the prosecutor. The names are all engraved. They had won a battle as great as any English naval victory.

William strode up to the bench, said he was free and prepared to go, only to be told he must remain prisoner until he paid his fine for contempt of court. He refused and was returned to Newgate.

The news travelled faster than today's post. Within hours the admiral at Wanstead had paid the fine, accompanied by a letter which informed William his father had only a few hours to live. The unexpected news shocked William into realising he loved and admired his father even more than his own firm principles. He rode his horse into a lather to get home in time. Father and son met in perfect amity. Each recognised in the other a born fighter who would never yield to the enemy. During the few remaining days of the admiral's life, William never left his father's side, nor did his grieving mother. In the course of those days the king and the Duke of York both called on the admiral and in Granville Penn's words, 'He had the comfort of receiving both from the king and the Duke of York the most gracious and kind assurance of their regard, and their promise of continuing the same to his son. A promise which both these princes religiously observed.' Penn expired at Wanstead on 16th September, not yet fifty years old, but aged and wasted by wars abroad and travail at home.

All during his life the admiral had worried about the financial fate of his widow, and had taken care to ensure that, in the event of his being killed, the government would ensure that she was cared for. In his will, a copy of which is still in existence, he did his best to ensure no financial trouble would add to her grief. He wrote,

> And first I doe will and devise unto my deare Wife Dame Margaret Penn to be paid unto her immediately after my decease the summe of Three hundred pounds sterling together with all my jewels other than what I shall hereinafter devise . . . the use during her life of one full moiety of all my plate . . . and all Coaches and Coach-horses or Coach-mares.

He knew William had no use for sword, guns or jewels, so left them to Richard and gave William his gold chain and medal presented to him by parliament. He left money to grand-daughter Margaret Lowther, but not to his rich daughter Peg Lowther. He remembered his nephews and his cousin William Penn and his worthy friend, Sir William Coventry, who was to be arbiter should differences arise.

Composing his *Vindication of his Deceased Father*, William went carefully through all his father's papers and found many a sigh of regret at the loss of the 'wise and friendly admiral'. From Chatham Shipyard, official report ended with an expression of sorrow and a Captain Sharland lamented that 'when General Penn was alive he had friends among the navy commissioners, but now he had none there'.

Even his enemies were prepared to be magnanimous now. England expected a state funeral. But 'Bury me by my mother' had been his reply when his wife spoke of Monck's state funeral a few months before. The wish for a private interment in the family parish church had been expressed in Penn's will of the previous year: 'to be buried in the parish church of Redcliffe within the city of Bristol as near the body of my deare mother deceased whose body lies there interred as the same conveniently may be.' Penn was modest even in his final aspirations.

It was a sad cortège that drove the long, weary miles from Wanstead to Bristol. It would have been less painful and quicker to have gone to the abbey, but to Margaret, her husband's wishes were law, and so they jolted their way down the familiar road which they had travelled frequently all their lives: London, Bristol and then often by sail to Ireland. If the admiral had more often sailed than ridden down to his port of departure there had been occasions like that when the widow had accompanied him by carriage to Portsmouth. He had been bound for Jamaica and she had written to him describing how the carriage had over-turned on the homeward route near Guildford. She could write to him no more. But she could see that his wishes were honourably carried out to the letter. He was buried immediately next to his mother, beneath a large black stone in the south transept in the church of St Mary Redcliffe, Bristol, universally acknowledged in its time to be, as Queen Elizabeth had said, 'the fairest, goodliest and most famous parish church in England.

The following account of his funeral, from a document preserved in the College of Arms, shews the high cavalier party of the day totally averse to honour, unwilling to recognise any professional merit displayed during the suspension of the crown:

To Captain Robert Challoner, Lancaster Herald. Sir, This day, Sir William Penn was interred in this city, at Ratcliffe Church. The manner of the solemnity was thus: after three or four companies of foot were passed, there were carried three large streamers, with his arms quartered therein: next to that his shield and gauntlets; then came the corpse, drawn with six horses; and at his head a red flag (as one of Oliver's generals, as it is said) and a white flag of the other according to the ships and squadrons he had served in, for the parliament, or for his majesty since his restoration; but whether these could be carried I know not neither; all which I believe are to be hanged up in the church. A herald painter came down with the hearse; but he brought no license or deputation from Sir Edward

Birch or Sir Edward Walker, as Sir Edward deputy here told me. Now, if he hath done more than can be justified you may improve it as you see cause, concealing my name. My thoughts are it is not right, nor could these flags be carried by one who had been against his majesty. Sir, etc. Ri. Ellsworth. College Green in Bristol. Sept 30th, 1670.

This spiteful letter had no effect. High up on the north wall is the memorial tablet to Sir William Penn. The wording was composed by his son William. It is framed by three streamers that he had flown from his ships, the blue, the white and the red, all of which have lost their colour. The fourth flag was the red flag of one of Cromwell's generals. The armour says much for the admiral's physical strength, for the total weight of such armour would be in the region of sixteen to twenty pounds, though, according to the Master Armourer of the Tower of London it was unusual for high-ranking officers to wear more than a cuirasse. But the admiral fought differently from most land-generals at sea, for he frequently led his men, jumping down to the deck of the enemy which was lower than his own. Surely, when he engaged in hand-to-hand combat, he must have worn the whole armour, or how else did he so miraculously escape ever being wounded?

The inscription on the tablet reads as follows:

To Ye Just Memory of Sr Will Penn Kt and Sometime Generall borne at Bristol in 1621 son of Captain Giles Penn several years consul for ye English in ye Mediterranean of ye Penns of Penns Lodge in ye County of Bucks and bye his mother from ye Gilberts in ye County of Somerset. Originally from Yorkshire. Addicted from his youth to maritime affairs. He was Captain at ye years of 21. Rear Admirall of Ireland at 23, Vice-Admirall of Ireland at 24. Admirall to ye Straightes at 29. Vice Admirall of England at 31. A Generall in ye First Dutch Warres at 32 whence retiring in Anno 1655. He was chosen a Parliament man for ye Towne of Weymouth 1660 made Commissioner of ye Admiralty and Navy Governor of ye Townes and Forts of King-Sail Vice Admirall of Munster and a member of that Provincialle Counsell and in Anno 1664, was Chozen Great Captain Commander under his Royal Highness; in ye signal and most Evidently

SUCCESSFUL FIGHT AGAINST THE DUTCH FLEET

Thus he took his Leave Of the Sea in his old element, But Continued still His other Employs till 1669; at which time Through bodily Infirmitys (Contracted by ye care and Fatigue of Public Affairs) He Withdrew Prepared and Made for his end, and with a gentle and Even Gale in much peace arrived and anchored in his Last and Best Port, at Wanstead in Ye County of Essex ye 16 September 1670 being then but 49 and 4 months old.

To whose Name and Merit his surviving Lady
Hath erected this Remembrance

Penn's passing was in keeping with the tenor of his life. His self-effacing funeral, his modest memorial, were thoroughly characteristic of the man. It was, in part, his own choice, in part the machinations of his enemies, that gave him a correspondingly modest share in the historical record. His place in history, by contrast, is a proud one and it is time to adjust the record to reflect it. On his achievements in command it is unnecessary to insist: the quality of his victories, especially in the conquest of Jamaica and in the Dutch wars, speaks for itself. Of his contribution to England's naval tradition, of his legacy to England and America, the evidence is eloquent enough.

But what sort of man was he? Glimpsed through the pages of Clarendon or Pepys, he appears a reprobate: an unprincipled trimmer, a corrupt time-server, a tipsy buffoon, a failed dynast. In none of these travesties is Penn genuinely recognisable. Far from changing allegiance opportunistically, he was constant, as we have seen, throughout the Civil War, Commonwealth, Protectorate and Restoration, to the old ideal of a mixed polity, of king and parliament combined, which had been expressed and sworn in *The Seaman's Protestation.* He stayed at the helm, through changes of régime, in defence of England, out of patriotism, not partisanship.

The imputation of corrupt practice was an occupational hazard for a Navy Board man; admirals 'that stole the sailors' bread' were so common in the period that honesty, being unexpected, was easily overlooked. Yet the evidence of Penn's exceptional probity is overwhelming. He amassed no fortune, save by way of grants of lands in forfeit; the rumours with which Pepys strews his *Diary* raise the presumption that Penn was all too scrupulous for his colleague's taste; his conduct over the Mediterranean prize in 1652 was manifestly exemplary; the charge that he acted improperly over the India prizes of

1665 was trumped up by malice; and his choice to be naval victualler at a time of general excitement against prevailing corruption shows where his reputation truly lay.

His 'merriness' should rather be seen as an endearing quality than as a vice. Only in the eyes of a jealous detractor or an unbending puritan could gaiety and conviviality be thought incompatible with morality. The strength of Penn's protestant convictions and the depth of his devotional life are attested by almost every page of his surviving writings and every act of his recorded life. We know of the atmosphere and tolerance and piety maintained, with Margaret's help, in his household, and of its effects on young William Penn; we know of the hospitality the Penns accorded to preachers; we may cite the radical protestant preferences evinced by the couple when they married; above all we may refer to the moving invocations of providence that fill Penn's letters and despatches and animate the verses, quoted above, which he wrote. His relations with his son, turbulent as they were, suffered from no divine insensibility or deficiency of fatherly feeling on Penn's part Rather, as we have seen, they were riven through and redeemed by love. The difficulties arose inevitably from a social context hostile to the reception of Quakerism by an admiral's son, and from the problems of psychological adjustment which the young Quaker had to overcome before reconciling his new vocation with his filial duty.

Finally, the most persistent claims – that Penn's life was devoted to self-exaltation and that his only constant aims were to found a great patrimony and acquire a title – collapse, as I have argued, from sheer lack of evidence. Only tittle-tattle, wildly elaborated by speculative historians, can be alleged in their support. The core of the theory – Penn's alleged interest in a country mansion – is contradicted by the very evidence, in Pepys's *Diary,* which is cited in its favour.

It is easy to dismiss all these false characterisations of Penn, hard to present a true portrait in its place. His greatest failings were in politics. He fared better than some friends: Sir Henry Vane went to the scaffold, the younger Pett to undeserved disgrace. Ormonde was under a cloud when Penn died; Batten was dead and his family impoverished; Broghill was alienated from his old comrades. Penn was powerless to influence any of this. He had failed to foresee the campaign against himself; he was compelled to suffer tamely imputations against his honour and his exclusion from command. So uncertain was he of his friends, that he was even prepared to believe, on very partial evidence, that the Duke of York had turned against him. Only royal patronage, which he had won by merit, not by manoeuvre, saved him from total destruction by his ruthless cavalier foes. He was doomed, by his political inexpertise, to watch the disaster of the Medway from the shore, and all his good service and good advice were insufficient to prevent it.

If he failed in politics, it was not because he was ignorant, as Pepys claimed, but innocent. Because he sought no political reward, he neglected the political arts and left himself exposed to the mischief of the great manipulators. In a sense, Pepys came close to an understanding of Penn when he reviled him as 'a common sailor'. For Penn was a tarpaulin at heart, a practical seaman, whose sagacity and humanity had been schooled at sea and were most at home in their own element. Landsmen cheated him, at the end of his life, of a place on the crest of the wave; perhaps now, long as it is after his death, the tide of history will restore him to a safe mooring in the haven of fame.

Select List of Printed Works

I. SOURCES

W. C. Abbot, ed., *Writings and Speeches of Oliver Cromwell* (4 vols, 1937–47)

A Great Victory Obtained by the English Against the Hollanders (1653)

A Great . . . Victory Obtained by the English Forces under the Command of General Penn and Gen. Venables against the French and others in the West Indies (1655)

A Letter from the Fleet with a Diurnal Account (1653)

Another Great Victorie Obtained by Vice-Admiral Penn against the Hollanders (1653)

R. C. Anderson, ed., *Journals and Narratives of the Third Dutch War* (1946)

Bloody Newes from Sea (1652)

Calendar of the Journals of the House of Lords (1810)

Calendar of State Papers, Colonial Series, 1547–1671, ed. W. N. Sainsbury (1860)

Calendar of State Papers: Domestic Series, 1625–70, ed. J. Bruce et al. (45 vols, 1858–97)

Calendar of State Papers: Ireland, 1633–70, ed. R. P. Mahaffy (7 vols, 1901–10)

Calendar of State Papers: Venetian, 1617–70, xv–xxvi, ed. A. B. Hinds (1909–37)

Charles I, *Whereas his Majesty, in consideration of the great merit and fruitful services of Sir William Penn*, etc. (Declaration assigning Pennsylvania to William Penn) (1861; facsimile ed. 1965)

– *The Letters, Speeches and Proclamations of Charles I*, ed. C. Petrie (1968)

C. H. Firth, ed., *The Narrative of General Venables* (1900)

C. H. Firth and R. S. Rait, *Acts and Ordinances of the Interregnum* (3 vols, 1911, 1982)

S. R. Gardiner and C. T. Atkinson, *Letters and Papers relating to the First Dutch War* (6 vols, 1899–1930)

A. Grey, *Debates of the House of Commons . . . 1667 to . . . 1694* (10 vols, 1769)

P. Hoste, *L'Art des armées navales* (1697)

– *Naval Evolution or a System of Sea-Discipline*, trans. C. O'Bryen (1762)

T. B. Howell, ed., *State Trials*, vi (1816)

E. Hyde, Earl of Clarendon, *The History of the Rebellion and Civil Wars in England*, ed. W. D. Macray (6 vols, 1888)

James II, *Memoirs of the English Affairs* (1729)

– *The Memoirs of James II*, ed. A. Bryant (1962)

Journals of the House of Commons, 1640–87, ii–ix (1803)

Journals of the House of Lords, 1628–75, iv–xii (1771–1836)

E. Ludlow, *Memoirs*, ed. C. H. Firth (2 vols, 1894)

C. McNeill, ed., *The Tanner Letters* (1943)

Manuscript Journals of the Long, Little, etc. Parliaments, ed. J. Bowdouin (1830)

Narrative of the Late Engagement between the English Fleet under . . . Blake, and the Holland Fleet under . . . Admiral Trump (1652)

S. Pepys, *The Diary of Samuel Pepys*, ed. R. C. Latham and W. Matthews (11 vols, 1970–83)

– *Further Correspondence*, ed. J. R. Tanner (1929)

– *Private Correspondence*, ed. J. R. Tanner (1926)

– *Naval Minutes*, ed. J. R. Tanner (1926)

G. Penn, *Memorials of the Professional Life and Times of Sir William Penn* (2 vols, 1833)

W. Penn, *My Irish Journal,* ed. I. Grubb (1952)

– *No Cross, no Crown* (1930, 1981)

– *The Sandy Foundation Shaken* (1668)

W. Penn and W. Mead, *The Trial of William Penn and William Mead at the Old Bailey* (1670)

– *Truth Rescued from Imposture* (1670)

J. R. Powell, ed., *The Letters of Robert Blake* (1937)

J. R. Powell and E. K. Timmings, eds, *The Rupert and Monck Letter Book, 1666* (1969)

F. J. Routledge, ed., *Calendar of the Clarendon State Papers* (1872)

J. Rushworth, *Historical Collections of Private Passages of State* (8 vols, 1721–22)

J. R. Tanner, *A Descriptive Catalogue of the Naval Manuscripts in the Pepysian Library* (1903)

The Life of Cornelius van Tromp (1697)

The Seaman's Protestation (1642)

The Seaman's Protestation Renewed, Confirmed and Enlarged (1643)

J. Thurloe, *A Collection of the State Papers of John Thurloe, Es.* (7 vols, 1742)

K. Tromp, *Leven en Bedryf . . . van M. H. Tromp* (1692)

Waerachtig ende perfect verhael, aegaende de Zee-Batallie . . . tusschen . . . Tromp ende . . . Blaeck, Penn etc. (1653)

B. Whitelock, *The History of England or Memorials of the English Affairs* (3 vols, 1713)

– *Memorials of the English Affairs* (4 vols, 1853)

II.   SECONDARY WORKS

W. Andrews, ed., *Bygone Essex* (1892)

M. Ashley, *Financial and Commercial Policy under the Cromwellian Protectorate* (1962)

– *Rupert of the Rhine* (1976)

H. Barbour, *The Quakers in Puritan England* (1964)

G. L. Beer, *Origins of the Old Colonial System* (1908)

J. Besse, *A Collection of the Sufferings of the People called Quakers* (2 vols, 1753)

P. J. Blok, *Life of Admiral De Ruyter,* trans. G. L. Renier (1933)

C. R. Boxer, *The Anglo-Dutch Wars of the Seventeenth Century* (1974)

– *The Dutch Seaborne Empire* (1965)

A. Bryant, *Pepys* (3 vols, 1938)

J. Campbell, *A Letter to a Friend in the Country* (1742)

G. N. Clark, *The Later Stuarts* (1934)

W. Laird Clowes, *The Royal Navy* (7 vols, 1903)

S. Colliber, *Columna Rostrata, or a Critical History of the English Sea-Affairs* (1727)

– *A Critical History of the English Sea-Affairs* (1742)

J. Corbett, *England in the Mediterranean, 1603–1703* (2 vols, 1904)

– *Monck* (1889)

G. Davies, *The Restoration of Charles II* (1949)

J. D. Griffith Davies, *Honest George Monck* (1936)

R. Davis, *The Rise of the English Shipping Industry* (1962)

W. H. Dawson, *Cromwells Understudy* (1938)

W. H. Dixon, *Robert Blake* (1856)

– *William Penn* (2 vols, 1872)

G. Edmondson, *Anglo-Dutch Rivalry during the First Half of the Sixteenth Century* (1911)

M. B. Endy, *William Penn and Early Quakerism* (1973)

C. H. Firth, *The Last Years of the Protectorate* (2 vols, 1909)

G. Fisher, Barbary Legend (1957)

A. Fraser, *Cromwell: Our Chief of Men* (1973)
– *King Charles II* (London, 1979)
S. R. Gardiner, *A Student's History of England* (3 vols, 1885–91)
– *History of the Commonwealth and Protectorate* (4 vols, 1903)
– *History of the Great Civil War* (4 vols, 1894)
S. R. Gardiner, ed., *Prince Rupert at Lisbon* (1902)
P. Gregg, *King Charles I* (1981)
D. Hannay, *A Short History of the British Navy* (1909)
P. H. Hardacre, *The Royalists During the Puritan Revolution* (1956)
L. A. Harper, *The English Navigation Laws* (1939)
A. Harris, *Edward Montagu, Earl of Sandwich* (1912)
R. W. Harriss, *Clarendon and the English Revolution* (1983)
O. F. G. Hogg, *Further Light on the Ancestry of William Penn* (1964)
G. D. M. Howat, *Stuart and Cromwellian Foreign Policy* (1974)
A. D. Innes, *Maritime and Colonial Expansion of England under the Stuarts* (1931)
H. M. Jenkins, 'The Family of William Penn',*Philadelphia Magazine of History and Biography,*
    xx, no. 1 (1896)
J. R. Jones, *Britain and Europe in the Seventeenth Century* (1966)
J. R. Jones, ed., *The Restored Monarchy* (1979)
P. M. Kennedy, *The Rise and Fall of British Naval Mastery* (1976)
J. P. Kenyon, ed., *The Stuart Constitution* (1966)
J. Latimer, *The Annals of Bristol in the Seventeenth Century* (1900)
– *The History of the Society of Merchant Ventures of the City of Bristol* (1903)
M. Lewis, *England's Sea-Officers* (1939)
T. H. Lister, *Life and Administration of Edward, 1st Earl of Clarendon* (1838)
A. T. Mahon, *The Influence of Sea Power upon History* (1890)
G. J. Marcus, *A Naval History of England,* i (1961)
P. Mathias and A. W. H. Pearsall, *Shipping: a Survey of Historical Records* (1971)
D. Nicholas, *Mr Secretary Nicholas* (1955)
D. Ogg, *England in the Reign of Charles II* (1934)
R. Ollard, *Man of War: Sir Robert Holmes and the Restoration Navy* (1969)
– *Pepys* (1974)
M. Oppenheim, *History of the Administration of the Royal Navy, 1509–1660* (1896)
C. O. Peare, *William Penn* (1966)
A. W. H. Pearsall, *The Second Dutch War* (19)
C. D. Penn, *The Navy under the Early Stuarts* (1913)
A. L. Pontalis, *John de Witt* (2 vols, 1885)
A. Pound, *The Penns of Pennsylvania and England* (1932)
J. R. Powell, *Robert Blake, General-at-Sea* (1972)
– *The Navy in the English Civil War* (1962)
M. Prestwich, *Cranfield* (1966)
R. W. Ramsey, *Henry Cromwell* (1933)
– *Richard Cromwell* (1935)
P. G. Rogers, *The Dutch in the Medway* (1970)
E. S. Roscoe, *Penn's Country and Other Buckinghamshire Sketches* (1914)
E. M. G. Routh, *Tangier* (1912)
J. H. S. Rowland, *Mr Pepys of the Navy* (1969)
V. A. Rowe, *Sir Henry Vane the Younger* (1976)
J. C. Ridley, *The Roundheads* (1976)
H. R. Rowen, *John de Wit* (1978)
Sir William Penn, Knight, Admiral and General at Sea, Great Captain Commander of the Fleet (1876)
J. R. Tanner, *English Constitutional Conflicts* (1928)

– *Samuel Pepys and the Royal Navy* (1920)
– 'The Anglo-Dutch Wars', *Cambridge Modern History,* v (1902)
– *'The Navy of the Commonwealth and the First Dutch War',* Ibid, iv (1902)
S. A. G. Taylor, *The Western Design* (1969)
A. W. Tedder, *The Navy of the Restoration* (1916)
The Penn Country of Buckinghamshire (1933)
J. Thirsk, ed., *The Restoration* (1976)
H. C. Tomlinson, *Guns and Government: the Ordnance Officer under the Later Stuarts* (1979)
A. Tully, *William Penn's Legacy* (1977)
D. Underdown, *Royalist Conspiracy in England* (1960)
R. T. Vann, *The Social Development of English Quakerism* (1969)
J. M. Wallace, *Destiny his Choice: the Loyalism of Andrew Marvell* (1968)
C. V. Wedgwood, *King Charles I* (1949)
– *Oliver Cromwell* (1973)
– *The Great Rebellion* (2 vols, 1978)
J. Willcock, *Life of Sir Henry Vane the Younger* (1913)
L. A. Wilcox, *Mr Pepys' Navy* (1966)
C. Wilson, *England's Apprenticeship* (1984)
– *Profit and Power: a Study of England and the Dutch Wars* (1957)
– *The Dutch Republic* (1968)
J. Wilson, *Fairfax* (1985)

Index

Index

DATE DUE

GAYLORD			PRINTED IN U.S.A